COMPETING
SPECTACLES

Other Crossway books by Tony Reinke

12 Ways Your Phone Is Changing You (2017)

Lit: A Christian Guide to Reading Books (2011)

Newton on the Christian Life: To Live Is Christ (2015)

"Thirty years after Neil Postman's *Amusing Ourselves to Death*, Tony Reinke's *Competing Spectacles* takes the impact-analysis of modern media to new levels. The conception of this book is not cavalier; it is rooted in the profound biblical strategy of sanctification by seeing (2 Cor. 3:18). The spectacle of Christ's glory is 'the central power plant of Christian sanctification.' Ugly spectacles make us ugly. Beautiful spectacles make us beautiful. Reinke is a good guide in how to deflect the damaging effects of digital images 'in anticipation of a greater Sight.'"

John Piper, Founder and Teacher, desiringGod.org; Chancellor, Bethlehem College & Seminary; author, *Desiring God*

"This book shows us how to pull our eyes away from the latest viral video or our digital avatars of self and toward the 'spectacle' before which we often cringe and wince: the crucifixion of our Lord. That's the spectacle we need."

Russell D. Moore, President, The Ethics & Religious Liberty Commission of the Southern Baptist Convention

"*Competing Spectacles* not only diagnoses our distorted vision; it prescribes spectacles that give us twenty-twenty spiritual vision. Essential reading."

Sinclair B. Ferguson, Chancellor's Professor of Systematic Theology, Reformed Theological Seminary; Teaching Fellow, Ligonier Ministries

"As a millennial who desires to abide in Christ while simultaneously engaging culture, I found this book incredibly helpful. The world seeks to captivate our attention through an endless stream of distractions, but Reinke encourages us to revive our hearts to the spectacle of Christ. I walked away encouraged to gaze upon the glory of the gospel, knowing it will reverberate through me and empower me to walk in Christlikeness."

Hunter Beless, Host, *Journeywomen* podcast

"Leaning on Scripture as the lens through which we view this digital age, Tony Reinke communicates in brilliantly lucid prose a proposal for how we can glorify our unseen Savior in this world full of sensory diversions."

Bruce Riley Ashford, Professor of Theology and Culture, Dean of Faculty, and Provost, Southeastern Baptist Theological Seminary

"If this book helps readers to digitally detox and to unplug from all sources of media that threaten to drown us in noise and to rob us of the capacity to attend to the things that truly enable us to flourish as human beings, then it will only have begun to do its good work."

W. David O. Taylor, Assistant Professor of Theology and Culture, Fuller Theological Seminary

"How to navigate the Christian life in a media-saturated culture feels more confusing than ever. Tony Reinke provides a dose of desperately needed clarity."

Jaquelle Crowe, author, *This Changes Everything: How the Gospel Transforms the Teen Years*

"Tony Reinke issues a grace-filled and prophetic call to examine ourselves as we navigate through a world of endless entertainment, spectacle, and distraction."

Trevin Wax, Director for Bibles and Reference, LifeWay Christian Resources; author, *This Is Our Time*; *Eschatological Discipleship*; and *Gospel-Centered Teaching*

"*Competing Spectacles* can guide us back to reality, honesty, and calm, as we lift our eyes humbly to the Crucified One and pray, 'Please show me *your* glory.'"

Ray Ortlund, Lead Pastor, Immanuel Church, Nashville, Tennessee

"Tony Reinke offers a succinct exposé of the threat that our image-saturated society poses to faith and to wisdom. We'll do well to heed his message."

Craig M. Gay, Professor, Regent College; author, *Modern Technology and the Human Future* and *The Way of the (Modern) World*

COMPETING SPECTACLES

Treasuring Christ in the Media Age

Tony Reinke

CROSSWAY®

WHEATON, ILLINOIS

Competing Spectacles: Treasuring Christ in the Media Age

Copyright © 2019 by Tony Scott Reinke

Published by Crossway
        1300 Crescent Street
        Wheaton, Illinois 60187

Cover design: Micah Lanier

First printing 2019

Printed in the United States of America

Unless otherwise indicated, Scripture quotations are from the ESV® Bible (The Holy Bible, English Standard Version®), copyright © 2001 by Crossway, a publishing ministry of Good News Publishers. Used by permission. All rights reserved.

Scripture quotations marked KJV are from the *King James Version* of the Bible.

Scripture references marked NIV are taken from The Holy Bible, New International Version®, NIV®. Copyright © 1973, 1978, 1984, 2011 by Biblica, Inc.™ Used by permission. All rights reserved worldwide.

Trade paperback ISBN: 978-1-4335-6379-9
ePub ISBN: 978-1-4335-6382-9
PDF ISBN: 978-1-4335-6380-5
Mobipocket ISBN: 978-1-4335-6381-2

Library of Congress Cataloging-in-Publication Data

Names: Reinke, Tony, 1977- author.
Title: Competing spectacles : treasuring Christ in the media age / Tony Reinke.
Description: Wheaton : Crossway, 2019. | Includes bibliographical references and index.
Identifiers: LCCN 2018040212 (print) | LCCN 2018056092 (ebook) | ISBN 9781433563805 (pdf) | ISBN 9781433563812 (mobi) | ISBN 9781433563829 (epub) | ISBN 9781433563799 (tp)
Subjects: LCSH: Christianity and culture.
Classification: LCC BR115.C8 (ebook) | LCC BR115.C8 R43 2019 (print) | DDC 261.5/2—dc23
LC record available at https://lccn.loc.gov/2018040212

Crossway is a publishing ministry of Good News Publishers.

LB   29 28 27 26 25 24 23 22 21 20 19
15 14 13 12 11 10 9 8 7 6 5 4 3 2 1

If then you have been raised with Christ,
seek the things that are above, where Christ is,
seated at the right hand of God.

—Colossians 3:1

Sheol and Abaddon are never satisfied,
and never satisfied are the eyes of man.

—Proverbs 27:20

O that I might see the joy that I desire.

—Anselm

CONTENTS

PART 2: THE SPECTACLE

PART 1

THE AGE OF THE SPECTACLE

§1: LIFE INSIDE THE DIGITAL ENVIRONMENT

Never in history have manufactured images formed the ecosystem of our lives. They do now. Sixty years ago Daniel Boorstin warned us: "We risk being the first people in history to have been able to make their illusions so vivid, so persuasive, so 'realistic' that they can live in them. We are the most illusioned people on earth. Yet we dare not become disillusioned, because our illusions are the very home in which we live; they are our news, our heroes, our adventure, our forms of art, our very experience."[1] Sixty years later, this risk is now our reality. We live as if all the media broadcast into our eyes is life itself, as if our images now offer us an alternative existence.

To this cultural phenomenon I raise my objection.

In a consumer society, images are the language of transaction. Images aim to provoke something in us in order to get something from us. New images ask us for all sorts of things—our time, our attention, our outrage, our money, our lust, our affection, and our votes. Is it possible to resist them? Should we try?

This book is a theology of visual culture, a culture that is increasingly closing in around us. It will not help you prioritize your TV options. Online viewing guides will help you there. It will not help you watch pop films through a gospel lens. Several good books do this already. Nor will it help you untangle the narrative threads of a thoughtful film.

---

1. Daniel J. Boorstin, *The Image: A Guide to Pseudo-Events in America* (New York: Vintage, 2012), 240.

Long conversations with friends are superior. More intentionally, this book is a companion for Christians walking through digital detoxes, the now necessary periods of our lives when we voluntarily unplug from pop media, news media, and social media in order to de-screen our eyes and to reorder our priorities.

As a convention, I must litter this book with two hundred footnotes.[2] On first read, ignore them and read slap through the book as if they didn't exist. Later you can return to the notes for deeper exploration.[3]

To keep the book brief, I painted my argument as one rough silhouette using a wide bristled brush and black paint on a white canvas. A much longer book could bring in a full spectrum of detail and color. Here I simply seek to answer one question: In this "age of the spectacle" (as it has been called[4])—in this ecosystem of digital pictures and fabricated sights and viral moments competing for our attention—how do we spiritually thrive?

---

2. Well yes, technically, they could have been endnotes in the back, but I'm a footnote guy.

3. No, really, ignore them.

4. Guy Debord, *La société du spectacle* (Paris: Buchet-Chast, 1967).

§2: SPECTACLES DEFINED

First we must clear up some definitions. *Spectacles* can mean one of two things. *Spectacles* are eyeglasses that sharpen human vision, bringing clarity as we look through them. In this sense, worldviews are metaphorical spectacles by which we see the world. But that is not how I will use the word. For this project, *spectacles* is confined to its second meaning: a moment of time, of varying length, in which collective gaze is fixed on some specific image, event, or moment. A spectacle is something that captures human attention, an instant when our eyes and brains focus and fixate on something projected at us.

In an outrage society like ours, spectacles are often controversies—the latest scandal in sports, entertainment, or politics. A spark bellows, grows into a viral flame on social media, and ignites the visual feeds of millions. That's a spectacle. As the speed of media grows faster and faster, the most miniscule public slip of the tongue or passive-aggressive celebrity comment or hypocritical political image can become a spectacle. And often the most viral social media spectacles are spicy tales later exposed as groundless rumors and fake news.[1]

Whether it's true, false, or fiction, a spectacle is the visible thing that holds together a collective gaze. And that's the focus of this book. A spectacle can come packaged as a brilliant photograph, an eye-catching billboard, a creative

---

1. Robinson Meyer, "The Grim Conclusions of the Largest-Ever Study of Fake News," theatlantic.com, March 8, 2018.

animation, a magazine centerfold, a witty commercial, or a music video. It can be an advertisement or a sarcastic anti-advertisement, a sitcom or a mocking anti-sitcom, a talk show or a cynical anti-talk show. Spectacles can go meta: TV shows about TV shows, ads about ads, and movies about movies. Spectacles are ambitious video-game landscapes, network television series, a blockbuster movie, a horror film, a sports clip of an athlete's glory (or injury), or a viral GIF on social media.

Spectacles can be accidental or intentional—anything that vies for our eyes: a historic presidential inauguration, a celebrity blooper, an epic fail, a prank, a trick shot, a hot take, a drone race, an eSports competition, the live streams of video games fought with fictional cannons, or real warfare fought with steel weapons. Spectacles are the latest video from a self-made YouTube millionaire sensation, or a flash mob meant to appear as a spontaneous gathering in public. And the age of spectacle making spawns a particular form of celebrity: the loudmouthed provocateur and the nitwit icon—notoriously unsuited for any other social role but fame.

Ad makers use premeditated spectacles to bolster corporate profits, but spectacles can have more grisly origins: a teen suicide on Facebook Live, a public assassination, a police-shooting video, or traffic footage of a deadly accident.

A spectacle can target you while simultaneously speaking to a million "yous" (like a popular video ad meant to coax purchases). Or a spectacle can gather together a community for a unified purpose (like a live political speech meant to coax votes). A particular tweet can become a viral spectacle, but the whole ecosystem of Twitter is one endless spectacle too.

Some spectacles draw us together in regional unity, like cheering for a local sports team. Others bring us together disconnectedly, like watching a movie in a theater. Some spectacles draw us together in small groups, like projecting movies on a TV in the living room. Some spectacles isolate us, like streaming Netflix on our iPad, scrolling social media on our phone, and gaming on a solo device. Some spectacles spatially separate us, like VR goggles.

Additionally, different modes of spectacle invite different forms of vision. Many spectacles, like our best movies, fixate our minds in a dream-like trance and put our bodies in a state of inertia. Some spectacles, like social media, offer a dopamine jolt as we become the center of attention. Other spectacles, like a TV show watched live and interacted with on Twitter, absorb us into a community of watchers. Spectacles can lead us to be self-centered or self-forgetting or others-focused. Others stoke our obscene voyeurism and personal lust.

Spectacles engage us differently. The Super Bowl is a supreme example, and it gathers our attention in different ways: live and in person, inside a stadium roaring with sixty thousand spectators; live and remotely, inside your living room with six friends; or on-demand, in the time-shifted medium of next-day highlights on your phone. The Super Bowl is also a prime example of how popular spectacles overlap. The event is a hybrid of athletic spectacles, celebrity spectacles, entertainment spectacles, and advertising spectacles—all generating mass interest for the latest consumables, devices, video games, and Hollywood releases. All the culture's most powerful spectacle makers meet at the Super Bowl, and even feed off one another, to create a four-hour, multilayered feast for the eyes.

Behind it all, spectacles want something from us. "Consuming" is part of it, but we don't merely ingest spectacles; we respond to them. Visual images awaken the motives in our hearts. Images tug the strings of our actions. Images want our celebration, our awe, our affection, our time, and our outrage. Images invoke our consensus, our approval, our buy-in, our respreading power, and our wallets.

§3: DISTRACTED SPECTACLE SEEKERS

Why do we seek spectacles? Because we're human—hardwired with an unquenchable appetite to see glory. Our hearts seek splendor as our eyes scan for greatness. We cannot help it. "The world aches to be awed. That ache was made for God. The world seeks it mainly through movies"[1]—and in entertainment and politics and true crime and celebrity gossip and warfare and live sports. Unfortunately, we are all very easily conned into wasting our time on what adds no value to our lives. Aldous Huxley called it "man's almost infinite appetite for distraction."[2]

Worthless or worthwhile, our eyes are insatiable things. And this visual appetite raises interesting questions about what attention is and how we should use it.

In the first volume of his landmark work *The Principles of Psychology*, William James explained the marvel and mystery of what it means to be an "attentive" being.[3] He said that human attention is a "withdrawal from some things in order to deal effectively with others, and is a condition which has a real opposite in the confused, dazed, scatterbrained state which in French is called *distraction*."[4]

Attention is the skill of withdrawing from everything to focus on some things, and it is the opposite of the dizziness of the scatterbrained spectacle seeker who cannot attend to

1. John Piper, twitter.com, April 12, 2017.
2. Aldous Huxley, *Brave New World Revisited* (New York: Harper & Row, 1958), 35.
3. William James, *The Principles of Psychology* (New York: Henry Holt, 1890), 1:402–58.
4. Ibid., 404.

anything. Thus, attention determines how we perceive the world around us. "Millions of items of the outward order are present to my senses which never properly enter into my experience. Why?" asks James. "Because they have no interest for me. My experience is what I agree to attend to. Only those items which I *notice* shape my mind—without selective interest, experience is an utter chaos."[5] James argued that of the many possible things that you could fix your mind on right now, you have chosen to attend to one thing—this sentence. Thus, this book is primarily shaping your life right now, not the one hundred other things around you that you must now ignore. That's attention. Which means that we must learn the art of refocusing a wandering mind, because "the faculty of voluntarily bringing back a wandering attention, over and over again, is the very root of judgment, character, and will."[6]

In other words, we're not simply creatures of our environment. We are creatures shaped by what grabs our attention—and what we give our attention to becomes our objective and subjective reality. Identical twins raised in an identical environment will be shaped differently if they focus on different things. We attend to what interests us. We become like what we watch.

---

5. Ibid., 402; emphasis added.
6. Ibid., 424.

§4: IMAGE IS EVERYTHING

Tennis superstar Andre Agassi was only nineteen years old when he starred in a television commercial for Canon cameras. The spot featured him in all sorts of eye-grabbing poses, a spectacle on display before the viewer's clicking shutter. As the ad closes, he steps out of a white Lamborghini in a white suit to speak his only line: "Image"—he says with a sly smile, pausing, tilting his head down to drop his sunglasses and to reveal his serious gaze—"is everything." The ad caught fire. Agassi said that he heard the slogan a couple times a day, then six times a day, then ten, then endlessly.

In his autobiography, he recounts his shock. The slogan stuck. He couldn't shake it. "Image is everything" *became* Agassi's image, one he spent years trying to escape. "Overnight," he said, "the slogan becomes synonymous with me. Sportswriters liken this slogan to my inner nature, my essential being. They say it's my philosophy, my religion, and they predict it's going to be my epitaph."[1] Crowds yelled the phrase at him whether he won or lost—because who needs tennis trophies when you can lose in style? The line mocked his tennis goals and minimized his athletic aspirations. It made him cynical, calloused to crowds, irritated by journalists, and eventually sickened by the public gaze. Perhaps Agassi was a victim, not so much of a scripted line but of a new impulse in the age of spectacles. *Image* and *substance*

---

1. Andre Agassi, *Open: An Autobiography* (New York: Vintage, 2010), 131–32.

were now divorced—because that is what images are: a simulacrum, a representation, an object that makes space between appearance and substance. "In a world dominated by the image instead of the word, interior life gives way to exterior show. Substance gives way to simulation."[2]

In the age of the spectacle, image is our identity, and our identity is unavoidably molded by our media. To use the evocative language of Jacques Ellul, speaking about movies, we choose to give ourselves vicariously to the on-screen lives that we could never personally experience. We escape into lives that are not ours and become adapted to the experiences of others. We live inside our projected simulations—inside the promises and the possibilities of our most beloved celebrities. The result, "like a snail deprived of its shell, man is only a blob of plastic matter modeled after the moving images."[3]

Our popular movies represent "a pedagogy of desire," a place where our loves and longings and identities are shaped for us.[4] In the age of the spectacle, we leave the hard edges of our embodied existence—our shells—in order to find our own shape and definition as we live inside a media-driven life of abstraction. And because we can live entirely inside the world of our images (consumed and projected), we lose our identity and our place in the community. We lose a sense of what it means to be inside the body God

2. Douglas Rushkoff in the afterword to Daniel J. Boorstin, *The Image: A Guide to Pseudo-Events in America* (New York: Vintage, 2012), 265.

3. Jacques Ellul, *The Technological Society* (New York: Vintage, 1964), 377.

4. James K. A. Smith, *Desiring the Kingdom: Worship, Worldview, and Cultural Formation*, vol. 1, *Cultural Liturgies* (Grand Rapids, MI: Baker Academic, 2009), 110.

assigned and shaped for us. Freed from the hard edges of our humanity, we become autonomous, plastic, shapeable blobs. "Digital technology abstracts society and creation from the particularity of our bodies, the material order, and our social situatedness, placing hypermodern selves within a thoroughly artificial environment of manipulated symbols and images."[5] We become detached selves, abstracted from nature and community—abstracted from our true selves.

All these media-driven identity confusions are amplified by the digital cameras on our phones, which arrived just in time to merge our self-image capture and our self-image editing in our social media.

---

5. Alastair Roberts, "The Strangeness of the Modern Mind," December 7, 2017, alastairadversaria.com.

§5: THE SPECTACLE OF THE SELF IN SOCIAL MEDIA

Today we get lost in a maze of mirrors that distort our reflections of the self, argues anthropologist Thomas de Zengotita. He says that our screen technology has grown to a new pinnacle of addictive delight in the digital age because our screens make it possible for us to live in a dual role: as both *spectator* and *star*.[1]

In the rare moments when we catch broad attention—whether through our images or tweets or memes—we become the *star*. And when we watch ourselves get approved and liked, we become the *spectator* too. In social media, our dual spectator-and-star role is seen "in the special intensity, the devotional glow you see on the face of a stranger in some random public place, leaning over her handheld device, utterly absorbed . . . matching twitter-wits on a trending topic, feeling the swell of attention rising around her as she rides an energy wave of commentary, across the country, around the world—it's like the touch of a cosmic force, thanks to the smallest and most potent of all personal screens, the one on her smartphone."[2] As we watch others watching us, we get caught up in the energy of becoming the star. We become spectators of our digital selves.

Our digital photos and selfies only amplify this self-projection. According to global stats, we now take more than one trillion digital pictures per year. We become actors before

1. Thomas de Zengotita, "We Love Screens, Not Glass," theatlantic.com, March 12, 2014.
2. Ibid.

our own phones and the phones of our friends. We modify our self and filter our appearance. And then we become spectators of ourselves, because "each selfie is a performance of a person as they hope to be seen by others."[3] As blobs, we seek an identity projection that others will celebrate.

Our camera-ready culture has changed us. Until 1920 no one thought it was appropriate to smile for a camera. Today we all must be ready to be photographed at any moment, ready to strike a performance pose contorted for the camera. Image is everything, and social media is where we craft the spectacle of ourselves. As we perform our self-chosen identities in front of our cameras, we find that the magic of computer-generated imagery (CGI) has been put in our hands. Our digital self is now editable by endless filters and lenses and bitmojis—a unique plasticity for self-sculpting offered to no other generation in human history.

After writing a book exclusively about smartphones and how they form and de-form our self-perception, I will not belabor the social media spectacle here.[4] What's important to see in this project is that self-sculpting and self-projecting make social media an irresistible spectacle because we become the self-molded star at the center of it all. As a result of these cultural shifts, we each feel the shift from *being* to *appearing*. Our self-made images—our digital appearings—become everything.

3. Nicholas Mirzoeff, *How to See the World: An Introduction to Images, from Self-Portraits to Selfies, Maps to Movies, and More* (New York: Basic, 2016), 62.

4. See Tony Reinke, *12 Ways Your Phone Is Changing You* (Wheaton, IL: Crossway, 2017).

In a deeply addictive way, we exist as both star *and* spectator. And social media "testifies to the power of that dual aspect of display, a reciprocal intimacy that no engagement with any other medium, let alone reality, can match."[5]

Well, only gaming comes close.

---

5. de Zengotita, "We Love Screens, Not Glass."

§6: THE SPECTACLE OF THE SELF IN GAMING

As Thomas de Zengotita points out, video games also situate us in the role of *spectator* and *star*, but those roles merge in realtime. "A seasoned gamer has mastered the console. He isn't conscious of his physical situation. He presses the buttons to turn and shoot and jump without thinking about them. He becomes the agent on the screen. There is no gap between his dirty little 14-year-old thumb and his avatar's massive biceps as it wields that enormous gatling gun against the zombie horde. He is the 'first-person shooter.'"[1]

Zengotita's tone is too dismissive, but his point is also too significant to ignore, especially as he goes on to explain the psychological effect. "As a first-person shooter, you get to perform *and* you get to watch at the same time," he says. "The powers and pleasures of two kinds of centrality—spectator and star—have merged. An untapped possibility for synaptic closure has been realized and an historically unprecedented form of human gratification attained. No wonder those games are addictive."[2] Yes, and on the verge of the VR (virtual reality) revolution, first-person shooter games set in open-world environments are only going to become more addictive, offering thrills in victory that were previously reserved for elite athletes.[3]

---

1. Thomas de Zengotita, "We Love Screens, Not Glass," theatlantic.com, March 12, 2014.

2. Ibid.

3. When one NBA player was asked to compare the thrill of a recent video game victory in Fortnite (a survival game against up to 99 other competitors) to the thrill of winning a NCAA college basketball championship two years earlier as the

But it's this same addictive quality that lures us back to social media on our smartphones, yet in a slightly offset way, in a dance between these roles as spectator and star. In social media "you also engage with yourself, with your world, on this new plane of being where agent and observer are fused. But the smartphone ups the ante. It introduces just enough distance, just enough lag time, between you and your doings on the screen to allow for an endless cascade of tiny moments of arrival, of recognition. Each prompt, each response, intercedes between you and the representations of yourself and your world that you are both producing and contemplating."[4] In social media, if we wait a moment, we get feedback, we get seen. We don't get the instant gratification of the gamer, but we come close.

In either case, whether it's in the live moment of gaming spectacles or in the slightly time-offset dance of social media, we stand at the center. We become star and spectator. In our most addictive media, we become the spectacle.

team's star, he had to think hard. Dan Patrick Show, "Lakers Guard Josh Hart Talks Fortnite & More with Dan Patrick," youtube.com, March 23, 2018.

4. de Zengotita, "We Love Screens, Not Glass."

§7: SPECTACLES OF TELE-VISION

The opening sequence of *The Simpsons* is now cultural legend. Parting through clouds to the sounds of heavenly chorus, we zoom in to Bart scrawling out his latest transgression on a school chalkboard. The bell rings, and he runs outside and jumps on his skateboard with no backpack or books. Next we see overachieving Lisa in an afterschool band practice, but her saxophone solo is too much, and the instructor points her out the door. She jumps on a bike and rides off with her instrument and a giant stack of books. At the town's nuclear power plant, the workday ends with a horn, at which Homer brainlessly drops a tong holding a glowing carbon core, which bounces and embeds in the back of his shirt as he walks off. He drives off, discovers the uncomfortable nuclear rod, discards it out the car window, and it bounces across the sidewalk as Bart dodges it on his skateboard. Next we see Marge and the pacifier-sucking toddler, Maggie, check out at the grocery store, then drive home in a screeching, horn-honking rush. The family races home from every direction. Homer pulls in the driveway first, then Bart, skateboarding over the roof of Homer's car. Angered, Homer steps out and lets out a screech as he's nearly run over by Lisa on her bike. He jumps and squeals again, then sprints inside the house to narrowly escape getting run over by his speeding wife, who slams on the brakes to make a skidding stop in the garage. In unison, the family sprints, jumps, and squeezes into place on the couch, in front of the blue glow of their shared TV—the family's eye-pacifier, it seems. We're meant to scoff at this dysfunctional household and the vanity of their daily existence—man, woman, underachiever, overachiever, toddler—each brainwashed by media, all gathered again before the comfort of their TV spectacles. But then, here we are, watching them. Are we the ones getting mocked?

So what has made the Simpsons blind to one another? Why do they only see through each other? And why do they avoid eye contact? Perhaps fed with endless offerings of video, our own gaze becomes easily numbed, blank, and bored. We ignore one another, and when we must make eye contact, too often we offer others a disinterested gaze. Maybe our spectacle culture has conditioned us to this place—"wooed several gorgeous hours a day for nothing but our attention, we regard that attention as our chief commodity, our social capital, and we are loathe to fritter it."[1] Television alone is worthy of our precious attention, and we protect that gaze from others. People become rather boring compared to the enrapturing magic of our screens.[2]

Tele-vision is the bringing of far-off things to our immediate vision. Beginning with video footage of the assassination of JFK, catastrophe came so close to us that we

---

1. David Foster Wallace, *A Supposedly Fun Thing I'll Never Do Again* (New York: Back Bay Books, 1998), 64.

2. "An imageless gaze at my friend's face can be cultivated only through a continual guard of the eyes; it has become a fought-for ideal that I can pursue only by constant training, behavior that runs counter to the surrounding *Bildwelt* [pictorial world] that solicits me to deliver myself to the show." Ivan Illich, "Guarding the Eye in the Age of Show," *RES: Anthropology and Aesthetics*, vol. 28 (Autumn 1995): 60.

could remember where we were standing, as if we stood in the presence of the tragedy and witnessed it for ourselves.[3] JFK's shooting, MLK's shooting, Reagan's shooting, Princess Diana's death, the Twin Towers collapse—you remember where you stood when you first witnessed video of these events. While first responders to 9/11 said it was like living inside a movie, *tele-vision* brought the movie-like catastrophe close to all of us. Through video, spatial separation dissolves, and far-off events are brought to our couches. Through video, we all become eyewitnesses to tragedy, brought so close to events that we feel present—so present that in the face of televised disaster we experience a mediated trauma of our own.

Video is now everywhere. Whatever happens in front of any other Wi-Fi–connected digital camera in the world can be mediated to us and to our vision. Amateur video is pouring into public platforms every second of the day. More than twenty-four thousand minutes of new *user video* is uploaded to YouTube every minute of every day. This means that the tonnage of *new video content* uploaded to YouTube in the next fifty-eight hours would require an unbroken lifespan of eighty years to watch.

Our insatiable appetite for *produced video* is mirrored in the expansive suite of our streaming platforms: Hulu, Netflix, Amazon Prime, Facebook video, YouTube Red, and several other video-on-demand and live-video streaming

---

3. Thomas de Zengotita, *Mediated: How the Media Shapes Your World and the Way You Live in It* (New York: Bloomsbury, 2005), 6–11.

platforms, most of whom not only host video but now fund their own studio projects.

The estimated number of running, scripted, original television series available on American television boomed from 210 in 2009 to 455 in 2016—an exponential growth with no signs of slowing down.[4] Cresting five hundred shows per year seems imminent. And that number doesn't include reality TV shows, 750 of which aired in 2015 alone.[5] Add to this watchlist the hundreds of movies released each year, with thirty or so of the most talked-about movies grossing ticket sales over $100 million.

New big-dollar spectacles compete for our attention. As I write this, on a random fall weekend, two blockbuster action movies, two new releases of mega-gaming franchises, and the second season of a streaming hit show were released on the same day. Big-money launches will continue to be the norm—multiple spectacles, with similar launch dates, all vying for the same eyes and leaving consumers on Twitter to express their blissful distress at prioritizing the attention demands.

Even our news has become more immersive over time. Scripted evening news programs—with tidy recaps of the day's major events, edited into one neat program—first gave way to the breaking news and endless live video feeds of CNN, and have now given way to Twitter. Now the raw

---

4. Maureen Ryan, "TV Peaks Again in 2016: Could It Hit 500 Shows in 2017?," variety.com., December 21, 2016.

5. Todd VanDerWerff, "750 reality TV shows aired on cable in 2015. Yes, 750," vox.com, January 7, 2016.

footage and earliest allegations and theories and eyewitness reports are delivered to us even before the event has ended. In Twitter, we all become reporters piecing together the story.

But there's no need to belabor the point that we live in a culture dominated by produced video and subsidized spectacles. The point is that all these increasing options are changing us. Whether we're talking about primetime dramas, reality TV, YouTube channels, breaking news, comedy routines, gaming franchises, or animated movies, "in a mediated world, the opposite of *real* isn't phony or illusional or fictional—it's *optional*."[6] The real world around us dissolves away, not because our spectacles are false or fake, but because we hold sovereign sway over a menu of endless spectacle options. We control it all. We remote-control it all. And inside the buffet of digital options, we lose sight of the edges that give shape to our embodied existence. We grow blind to what we cannot control.

In the *tele-visual* age, our eyes run to and fro throughout the whole earth in godlike omniscience, with endless options offered to us in our handheld phones. More easily than ever, spectacles reach us from the other side of the world. And while we may be in control of our private spectacles, we also become more passive to them. Spectacle resistance is an option we willfully ignore. Our lazy eyes and our incurious gaze are happily fed by the spectacle makers. We no longer seek out new spectacles; new spectacles seek

---

6. de Zengotita, *Mediated*, 14; emphasis added.

us out, delivered to us with hardly more required than a thumb twitch, or less. Auto-playing video clips animate, expire, and then scroll on to the next one in line. Auto-starting next episodes extend our Netflix bingeing. We are asked to do nothing. Simply veg.

Few of us have reckoned with the consequences of this tele-visual culture on our attention, our volition, our empathy, and our self-identity.

§8: SPECTACLES OF MERCHANDISE

The rise of both video spectacles and marketed consumables is no accidental marriage. Images capture our attention and lure us because they implicitly ask us to try on various costumes of identity, to envision how a product will craft our appearance in the eyes of others. And this manicured persona goes far deeper than cosmetics and clothing; it's the drive behind much of our consumable goods.

Chanon Ross describes the link between spectacle and consumption with the illustration of a mall shopper. "When a consumer enters the shopping mall, her senses are engaged by a panoply of stimuli designed to intoxicate. Images, music, scents, and products swirl together in a whirlwind of desire. The consumer does not have to want anything before entering the shopping mall because it is designed to cultivate desire *for her*, and it provides her with the products she needs to consummate the desire *it* has produced."[1] In our search to shape the formless blob of self-identity, we turn to new products. But outside the mall, the enchanted magic begins to lift, and soon the wardrobe looks drab. When it does, "purse in hand, she heads off once again to the shopping mall, and the cycle of de-intensification begins anew." The spectacle promises to give us an image others in the same culture will identify and appreciate, if we buy the right products. The promise is that "through his purchasing power, the consumer is able

1. All quotations in this paragraph are from Chanon Ross, *Gifts Glittering and Poisoned: Spectacle, Empire, and Metaphysics* (Eugene, OR: Cascade, 2014), 89–91.

to rise above the material world and experience himself as a transcendent being." But real life hits, and we feel our humanity, our fallenness, and the vanity of pleasure seeking in this world. The dull pangs of our emptied heart lure us back into the mall for more goods. But "ever-greater spectacles must be produced" to attract our attention. "Images must be more vivid, violence even more excessive, reality television more outrageous, political campaigns more dramatic, and so on." In this age of the de-intensifying spectacle, we must find fresher and brasher spectacles to recapture our prone-to-wander gaze.[2]

Spectacles of the advertisers are meant, like the mall, to awaken new desires within us that previously didn't exist until the lack of a consumer good was identified as the cause. The advertising spectacle "serves not so much to advertise products as to promote consumption as a new way of life."[3] Advertising spectacles create new itches inside us that can be scratched only by the next consumable good. The main function of the advertiser is "to awaken desire; to create, not to gratify thirst; to provoke a sense of lack and

2. Undergirding reality TV ratings is an "inhibition of shame," as contestants and producers are willing to do more and more bizarre things, says David Foster Wallace. In a post-shame world, it matters little if a controversial show draws wide scorn or rebuke, because "even if viewers are sneering or talking about in what poor taste stuff is, they're still watching, and that the key is to get people to watch, and that that's what's remunerative. Once we lost that shame hobble, only time will tell how far we'll go." Stephen J. Burn, ed., *Conversations with David Foster Wallace*, Literary Conversations (Jackson, MS: University Press of Mississippi, 2012), 132. People still tune in to see what they can only scoff and scorn, and on this basis even more absurdly premised reality TV shows are born.

3. Christopher Lasch, *The Culture of Narcissism: American Life in an Age of Diminishing Expectations* (New York: Norton, 1991), 72.

craving by giving us the apparent presence of something and taking it away in the same gesture."[4] The advertiser's goal is to "create an anxiety relievable by purchase."[5] A spectacle puts before our eyes an object of desire, provoking a new longing for satisfaction in the thing or the experience, and then swiftly tugs the object away from us, leaving us with a new thirst, a new craving, that must be quenched in the purchasing of the thing or experience.

Advertising spectacles build powerful habits within us and make us endlessly restless buyers who crave the power to change our lives and our surroundings with another trip to the mall. The blob of the autonomous self is promised a new identity in a shiny new exoskeleton—a new consumable good to complete us and give us form in the world, to shape the identity we want to project to others. So we become self-consumed consumers—autonomous buyers whose lives are given new shape and form by the next thing we add to our Amazon shopping cart.

For years, consumer products were validated by an "As seen on TV!" sticker. Visual spectacles substantiate consumables, and they still do. Ads work best the more people see them, and this is why we see the same ads cycle over and over and over. Ads are potent not merely because they reach a lot of eyes but because they shape how an entire culture views a product, a phenomenon called *cultural imprinting*. "Advertisers have power because goods that

---

4. W. J. T. Mitchell, *What Do Pictures Want?: The Lives and Loves of Images* (Chicago: University of Chicago Press, 2005), 80.
5. David Foster Wallace, *Infinite Jest* (New York: Back Bay Books, 2006), 414.

have an image associated with the mass spectacle register publicly as having a particular meaning," says theologian Alastair Roberts. "Seeing an ad privately is nowhere near as powerfully effective as seeing an ad in Super Bowl coverage, as in the latter case we know that everyone else has seen the same image and it has registered in the public awareness. Advertising and the spectacle feed into a culture of mutual display."[6] Every ad attempts to form a new longing within me, but the most prominent ads imprint a specific good as universally meaningful to us all. Then if I buy this marketed *thing*, I can assume that the whole culture will view me in a certain light.

In these ways the age of spectacles and the age of consumables merge naturally. Bluntly put, in the words of one theologian, our age is "a remarkably shrill and glaring reality, a dazzling chaos of the beguilingly trivial and terrifyingly atrocious, a world of ubiquitous mass media and constant interruption, a ceaseless storm of artificial sensations and appetites, an interminable spectacle whose only unifying theme is the imperative to acquire and spend."[7] Behind the age of the spectacle is the age of consumption. Fed by a diet of sugary sensational candy and cultural imprinting, we gain new appetites for the world we see, as we lose our taste for the unseen. And this is no random process. All our appetites and longings are discipled by the

---

6. Alastair Roberts, personal email, March 10, 2018, shared with permission. See also Kevin Simler, "Ads Don't Work That Way," meltingasphalt.com, September 18, 2014.

7. David Bentley Hart, *The Experience of God: Being, Consciousness, Bliss* (New Haven, CT: Yale University Press, 2014), 329.

world's spectacles so they can be pacified by an industry that reduces our desires to the newest goods and the next vacation and the latest consumer technology.

Spectacles make demands on us—they want our self-image, our time, our outrage, our attention, our hearts, our wallets, and, of course, our votes.

§9: POLITICS AS SPECTACLE

On election night, November 8, 2016, Hillary Clinton prepared herself to become the first woman president in United States history—an historic moment made certain by most of the national polls. Two days earlier, the *Los Angeles Times* confidently announced, "Our final map has [Hillary] Clinton winning with 352 electoral votes."[1] A runaway victory was the safe bet.

To host her unprecedented triumph, Clinton chose the Crystal Palace in New York City's Javits Center, a stunning six-block glass citadel with a crystal ceiling, a grand spectacle spring-loaded with the driving metaphor for Clinton's victory speech—breaking through the glass ceiling of a male-dominated political world and winning a victory for all women. Clinton's white suit was pressed and ready, the color to honor the work of suffragettes in a previous century. ("We had really gone the distance on the symbolism," she said later.[2]) Huge screens projected the latest electoral tally. Pop celebrities, face-painted supporters, and eager donors strolled the glass castle with an electricity of imminent victory. The stage was set, the lights were on, the podium stood ready. But as the evening wore on, Clinton's leads disappeared. At 8:15 p.m. Clinton was leading Florida. By 11 p.m. she had lost Florida. At 10:30 p.m. she lost Ohio. At 12:00 a.m. she lost Iowa. At 1:35 a.m. she lost Pennsylvania. By 2:30 a.m. it was over.

---

1. David Lauter and Mark Z. Barabak, "Our Final Map has Clinton Winning with 352 Electoral Votes," latimes.com, November 6, 2016.

2. Hillary Rodham Clinton, *What Happened* (New York: Simon & Schuster, 2017), 18.

She picked up the phone and conceded the election to her opponent. Her white suit was never unpackaged. One journalist on site likened the experience, not to watching a ceiling get blown off, but to being a passenger on the Titanic—a huge magnificent spectacle, with the bottom fallen out.[3]

If the previous presidential election in 2008 was hyped as a pinnacle of political spectacle making (which it was), it was a mere preamble to 2016 and the modern-day master of spectacle making, Donald Trump. I do not suggest that there was zero substance behind his person or his political ambitions or his business success, and clearly his message resonated with a vast swathe of America. Whether or not we agree with him, we must now reckon with the media muscle he employed to sway masses away from a political elite to himself, a political newcomer.

While most of the candidates raised and spent millions of dollars to buy airtime to play edited spectacles of themselves during commercial breaks, Trump garnered billions of dollars worth of free media coverage by making his unscripted speeches irresistible to the camera.[4] While the other presidential candidates bought ad slots for airtime breaks, Trump owned the airtime. By the time it was over, in election reporting, Trump's name was mentioned three times more often than Clinton's.[5]

3. Nathan Heller, "A Dark Night at the Javits Center," newyorker.com, November 9, 2016.

4. Nicholas Confessore and Karen Yourish, "$2 Billion Worth of Free Media for Donald Trump," nytimes.com, March 15, 2016.

5. According to "Presidential Campaign 2016: Candidate Television Tracker," television.gdeltproject.org, n.d.

During one of his signature "Make America Great Again" campaign rallies, ten thousand supporters turned out to see Trump in Harrisburg, Pennsylvania, a key state he needed to win (and did). From the campaign podium, he boldly admitted: "Now, my wife is constantly saying, 'Darling, be more presidential.' I just don't know that I want to do it quite yet. We have to be tough for a little while. At some point I'm going to be so presidential that you people will be so bored, and I'll come back as a presidential person, and instead of 10,000 people, I'll have about 150 people, and they'll say, 'But, boy, he really looks presidential!'"[6]

Donald Trump knew what he was doing. His staff was left to translate the strategy as a "theory of two Donalds." First, Trump would rouse apathetic voters by stirring them to action with tough talk and public spectacles on stage. Then he would get elected, pivot, and take up the decorum befitting a president. Worried conservatives, who feared that the Trump they saw on campaign stages would become the same Trump inside the Oval Office, were reassured that a pivot would happen and a second Trump would triumph in the end.[7]

Whether or not this proposed pivot happened, I leave to the reader. What I want to point out here was how, on his way to becoming president, Donald Trump deliberately and strategically trusted in his spectacle-making magic. Phase one was meant to capture the live, prime-time stage.

6. Donald Trump, rally in Harrisburg, Pennsylvania, April 21, 2016.
7. Josh Voorhees, "Team Trump Embraces the Theory of Two Donalds," slate.com, April 22, 2016.

With brief and blunt speeches, Trump attracted attention that no other candidate could match. If the whole thing appeared sloppy and undignified, it was the messy genius of a spectacle-making master. Trump knows that presidential decorum is now too small a furnace to fuel the power necessary to capture mass votes in the media age. Since video became a staple of American culture, the power of televised images of candidates has always proved an essential component of political momentum. But nothing could prepare us for how Trump would keep the cameras rolling and usher in a new age of political spectacle.

Trump evokes mass response by working from slogans, even simply repeating key phrases and mottos and branded indictments of his opponents. His language is blunt. His sentences are short. His slogans flow freely and naturally. He has mastered the viral tweet. On stage, he comes across as "perpetually annoyed—exasperated that things aren't as they should be—but somehow also good-humored about it," and that makes good television theatrics.[8]

For Trump, television is king. In the early days of his presidency, even his staffers reportedly found themselves surprised by how little Trump read. Some concluded: "Trump didn't read. He didn't really even skim. If it was print, it might as well not exist." Why not? White House staffers debated whether he struggled with some form of dyslexia. Or maybe he was semiliterate? "Others concluded

---

8. Barton Swaim, "How Donald Trump's Language Works for Him," washingtonpost.com, September 15, 2015.

that he didn't read because he just didn't have to, and that in fact this was one of his key attributes as a populist. He was postliterate—total television."[9]

In 2016, whether you loved Donald Trump, tolerated Donald Trump, or despised Donald Trump, you were swept into the spectacle of Donald Trump. He dominated video and converted his televised energy into political momentum. In the words of one report, his "ability to bring previously distinct forms of semiotic extravagance together (reality television, beauty contests, wrestling matches) and insert them into his candidacy for the most powerful position in the world is precisely what makes Trump a never-ending spectacle."[10] In response, you can voice your opposition and picket his rallies, but you only feed the fire and give the cameras more footage.

After Trump was elected, the American economy roared to life, and the Dow Jones soared to several new records in his first year. In the same span, the endless drama around his staff turnover was dubbed "the greatest reality show ever."[11] Whatever is finally made of the Trump presidency—whether he represents necessary change in America or a cultural mishap never to be repeated—one

---

9. Michael Wolff, *Fire and Fury: Inside the Trump White House* (New York: Henry Holt, 2018), n.p. This is a dubious book, but this point has been corroborated by more reputable news sources. See also Carol D. Leonnig, Shane Harris, and Greg Jaffe, "Breaking with Tradition, Trump Skips President's Written Intelligence Report and Relies on Oral Briefings," washingtonpost.com, February 9, 2018.

10. Kira Hall, Donna M. Goldstein, Matthew Bruce Ingram, "The Hands of Donald Trump: Entertainment, Gesture, Spectacle," *Hau: Journal of Ethnographic Theory* 6 (2): 92.

11. Chris Cillizza, "Donald Trump Is Producing the Greatest Reality Show Ever," cnn.com, March 6, 2018.

lasting change will be the newfound political power of the spectacle. The fireworks of political spectacle are the new pyrotechnics of political momentum. Perhaps the office of president is now best suited for the celebrity class, the masters of the spectacle.

§10: TERROR AS SPECTACLE

In the summer of 2013, as civil war tore apart his country, Bashar al-Assad, the president of Syria, allegedly fired chemical weapons against his opposition. The attack reportedly killed eighteen hundred men, women, and children in Ghouta, Syria.

The UN investigated the massacre and confirmed that the attack came from within Syria and that "significant quantities" of military-grade sarin gas were used "in a well-planned indiscriminate attack targeting civilian-inhabited areas, causing mass casualties."[1] One man, a rare survivor of the attack, likened sarin exposure to the lost ability to inhale, the inability to scream in pain at the body's natural urge, and a fight for each breath in excruciating agony, like someone was tearing his chest apart "with a knife made of fire."[2]

Such ruthless butchery of his own citizens sparked global outrage and condemnation of Assad. Threats of retaliation escalated. America prepared to strike back. A few days after the slaughter, business tycoon Donald Trump took to Twitter to ask President Obama: "What will we get for bombing Syria besides more debt and a possible long-term conflict?"[3] Lacking an international consensus, Obama stood down on military retaliation.

---

1. Human Rights Council of the United Nations, "Report of the Independent International Commission of Inquiry on the Syrian Arab Republic," OHCHR.org, February 12, 2014.

2. Ryan Gorman, "Syrian Sarin Attack Survivor Describes the Feeling of 'a Knife Made of Fire,'" businessinsider.com, April 20, 2015.

3. Donald J. Trump, twitter.com, August 29, 2013.

Thirteen hundred days later, and 150 miles to the north, Assad allegedly repeated his savagery, this time targeting Khan Sheikhoun, Syria, killing seventy-four of his civilians with another air strike of sarin gas.[4] Within sixty-three hours of the event, Donald Trump, America's new president, fired fifty-nine Tomahawk cruise missiles at a military airfield in Syria, turning one of Assad's fighter jet fleets into a pile of scorched rubble.

How do we explain Trump's pacifism to eighteen hundred dead in 2013 in light of his hawkish response to seventy-four dead in 2017? The short answer: *pictures*. Graphic pictures. More than the earlier episode, the latest action was captured by photographs of the children—with looks of surprise, fear, and confused suffocation frozen into their dead faces, then fixed into horrific images and videos that spread swiftly around the world.

Military officials collected the evidence and briefed Trump on the April 2017 attack. "The images were ghastly. Men and women gasping for breath. Small children foaming at the mouth and in agony. The lifeless bodies of babies sprawled on the ground." When the briefing ended, the president "dispatched his team to draw up options for a response." Those pictures could not be shaken. As he tried to go about his work, "the images from Syria weighed on him, his aides said. He was disturbed by

---

4. Assad quickly made his way to a televised interview to deny any involvement and to make the case that he did not have the materials, the capacity, or the motive to pull off this gas attack.

images of babies, some the ages of his grandchildren."[5] The images he saw—"more graphic than those the public had seen"—hit home.[6] He had to retaliate. And he did.

Trump's rapid response to this second Syrian attack reveals three powerful lessons about the visual spectacles of violence.

First, injustices against humanity captured by video need no translation. Pictures of dead children on sidewalks immediately captivate our eyes. Captions and descriptions may be typed in a foreign language, but the messages embedded in the images are universally spreadable.

Second, images are personally relatable. Videos and photographs of children on the street tap into the human heart of compassion. Once the images are shared and broadcasted, they etch the consciousness of all viewers. The images cannot be ignored.

Third, like never before, mobile digital cameras capture the optics of war crimes and spread them globally within seconds. A digital butterfly flaps its wings, and a digital tsunami of outrage gets unleashed on the other side of the planet within the hour. Within a few hours, collective rage can awaken war machines.

In the image-driven age, nothing is easier to weaponize than the collective indignation birthed from an enraging

5. Associated Press, "Ghastly Images of Syrian Attack Led to Trump About-Face," April 7, 2017.

6. Michael D. Shear and Michael R. Gordon, "63 Hours: From Chemical Attack to Trump's Strike in Syria," nytimes.com, April 7, 2017.

event captured on film. We now see this played out with regularity on all sides of a conflict. A radical terror group will create a graphic propaganda video featuring the gruesome executions of prisoners—shot, beheaded, burned, drowned, and documented for the world in HiDef color video. The shocked world responds to the images with hard talk from military brass and politicians on television talk shows.

The events of 9/11 brought video spectacles to a central place in warfare and national defense. We watched video of the Twin Towers collapsing into a dust pile. We watched a slightly tilted commercial airliner disappearing into the side of a skyscraper, emerging as a fireball on the other side, a hijacked missile fired into the heart of one of America's icons of wealth. These spectacles of horror, captured by cameras and looped over and over without end, burned into the global consciousness. The collective outrage was palpable and pointable and directable toward an enemy— if we had images of the terrorists behind it all.

To perpetuate a "war on terror," images of terrorists are key. Put faces to the atrocity and find footage of someone like Osama bin Laden. Brand him as "the enemy." This strategy works on the split screen of human attention—the towers falling on the left and video of the perpetrator on the right. The optics are essential, because without video footage, terrorists and their groups remain a nebulous and invisible force somewhere across the globe. Counterterrorism operations are often secret things, but politicians use public images to evoke fear and codify our most "imminent threats."

When it comes to the optics of warfare, we must use caution, but I'm not advocating for conspiracy theories. In fact, conspiracy theorists often manufacture a farcical version of a spectacle that leeches its power off a real event. In this case, there's little doubt that bin Laden was behind the 9/11 attacks, a masterful attempt to create "the greatest spectacle on earth" by assaulting grand icons of Western power. He and his associates performed these horrors, with a devastating outcome unparalleled in modern spectacle making. The images were the point because bin Laden did not set out to kill as many people as possible. He didn't need to. "He was prepared to make do with half the number of victims provided the towers were hit, and all the better if they collapsed. He wasn't waging a war that counted the enemy casualties; he was launching a message of terror, and what mattered was the image."[7]

Thanks to ubiquitous smartphones, terrorists can be assured that any spectacles of violence in major cities will be captured and shared around the world in real time. "The emergence of social media such as YouTube and Twitter has turned every citizen into a potential journalist, every innocent bystander into a potential witness whose testimony can be uploaded to the global nervous system."[8] All

---

7. Umberto Eco, *Chronicles of a Liquid Society* (Boston: Houghton Mifflin Harcourt, 2017), 113–14.

8. W. J. T. Mitchell, *Cloning Terror: The War of Images, 9/11 to the Present* (Chicago: University of Chicago Press, 2011), 130.

sides to the conflict know what this means. Images generate outrage that can be bottled and weaponized into a justifiable military response.

On April 5, one day after the Blackhawk reprisal by President Trump, the US Ambassador to the United Nations, Nikki Haley, spoke before a UN Security Council on Syria. There she held up two photographs of dead Syrian children (part of the collection of images that haunted the president). Pictures of Ms. Haley, a mother of two, holding up the images before photojournalists generated yet another wave of viral images in the media.

On April 13, with all this Syria-focused outrage in the air, the United States military took offensive and dropped a massive bomb on an ISIS terror compound in Afghanistan. In a flash, the GBU-43, aka MOAB, or the "Mother of All Bombs," became the most destructive nonnuclear bomb ever used in combat by the US military. It reportedly killed thirty-six ISIS operatives working inside an underground complex in a remote mountainous region. Within hours, the military released aerial footage of the explosion, a colorless and soundless video showing the visual reverberations of a blast radius that could be felt twenty miles away.

The next morning, the television talk program *Fox & Friends* opened a segment with the bombing footage, overlaid by Toby Keith's country song "Courtesy of the Red, White and Blue." As the pro-bombing, post-9/11–inspired lyrics ended, host Ainsley Earhardt added: "The video is

black-and-white, but that is what freedom looks like—
that's the red, white, and blue."[9]

For the cause of good or evil, both terrorism and anti-
terrorism feed energy off the optics. They exchange spectacles back and forth. The spectacles of a bloodbath by
kamikaze terrorists who spread carnage across populated
urban streets or inside malls or subway stations generate video footage that can be looped for hours on end.
And that footage will be used to help gather public anger
into the swift response of an anti-terror war machine.
The anti-terrorism war machine video response gener-
ates new B-roll optics for the terrorists to repackage into
their own propaganda. Both sides increase their power by
grabbing eyes.

Obviously, warfare is not the result of the age of video.
War is ancient. But today's warfare is justified, amplified,
extended, and magnetized to public sympathy and support
when the war (and the apparent enemy) can be fixed into
a visual spectacle and looped on national television to keep
the threat fresh in our eyes. War optics can turn the popu-
lous against the war machine (like we saw in Vietnam). But
war optics are also staged by the war machine, with high
voltage "shock and awe" spectacles made TV-ready. In the
media age, wars are battled not merely in isolated locations
around the world; they are battled in a format to fit the
theater of *everywhere*—in optics vying for airtime on the
ubiquitous screens in our pockets.

---

9. "Fox News Hosts Revel in Afghanistan MOAB Drop," axios.com, April 14, 2017.

Images trigger response. Images create impressions. But images are ambivalent. Images cannot carry an argument or imply a critical interpretation. We must bring the criticism ourselves. So every time we see spectacles of military power, or terror-driven bloodshed, we can ask ourselves: What do these images want from me? And who grows more powerful if I give it?

§11: ANCIENT SPECTACLES

Modern spectacle making isn't unique. The same tactics have endured for centuries. The ancient Greeks and Romans were both warrior cultures, both built around socially celebrated spectacles meant to showcase the ideal physique of its fighters and spawn new soldiers faithful to the realm. To these ends, the Greek stadium became famous for Olympic competitions and for endurance sports like running, wrestling, and boxing. The Roman arena was renowned for its gladiator fights, animal hunts, and public executions. While the Greeks were not bloodless (their boxing matches rival our MMA fights), neither were they modest. Their comfort with athletic nudity is notorious. But we remember the Romans for their greatest spectacle makers, the gladiators, made famous by their gratuitous bloodlust.

The Roman world was saturated by spectacle makers and spectacle consumers. By generating massive popular energy, spectacles became the engine driving political momentum and military enthusiasm. Marching your enemies through the city, before the jeers of the people, was a captivating military sight. And the gladiatorial games in the Colosseum united the politicians and electorate in a mass spectacle that created a feedback loop in which local political authorities could flex their spectacle-making power before an eager audience, and the audience could respond and participate in the directions of the games as a mass voice of approval or disapproval. Public spectacles translated into political and social power for Roman statesmen and aspiring politicians.[1]

These intoxicating Roman games and gladiator shows took over society. Gladiator fights, dramatic plays, exotic animal shows, thrilling circuses, military parades, public executions—the national life was lived through its theatrics.[2] And power players leveraged the whole charade for personal popularity. Entertainment, statecraft, worship, warfare, economics—it all merged together into one collective age of the spectacle, an interwoven social fabric expected to bear the weight of an empire.

1. Chanon Ross, *Gifts Glittering and Poisoned: Spectacle, Empire, and Metaphysics* (Eugene, OR: Cascade, 2014), 8.

2. Richard C. Beacham, *Spectacle Entertainments of Early Imperial Rome* (New Haven, CT: Yale University Press, 1999), 43–44.

§12: EVERY NINE SECONDS

We could argue that our spectacle age is not far removed from Rome, but our media has evolved with a few fresh features.

Samuel Morse, of Morse Code fame, sent the first telegraph message from DC to Baltimore in the spring of 1844. His message was a biblical exclamation: "What hath God wrought!" (Num. 23:23). We know what the telegraph wrought, a new opportunity to shrink data down into fragments and single sentences. The telegraph became the private text message, which became the public tweet. Today, all of our instantaneous social media has ushered in an age of scandal, celebrity gossip, and tweetstorms.

So while Imperial Rome celebrated its macrospectacles, what we face today is the rise of the microspectacle—tiny fragments of information, clips, phrases, and images, which can be spread at lightning speed across the globe. The faster our media delivery systems become, and the more efficiently those spectacles are delivered to the handheld devices in our pockets, the more viral phenomena shrinks into smaller and smaller microspectacles.

This spectacle compression is also possible because human attention can be split into nine-second moments. While it's not easy to measure, we all know that the human attention span is shrinking. Partly, we can blame the false promises of multitasking. And, partly, we can blame ourselves. It's our personal preference. Focusing our attention for too long is hard. Our brains love little snack breaks, and the digital media companies know it. We are targets of attention-candy that fits nicely into our appetite for something new, weird, glorious, hilarious, curious, or cute. Perhaps it's not too far from the truth to call the iPhone "a chemical-driven casino that preys on our base desires for vanity, ego, and our obsession with watching train wrecks."[1] We love the ego buzz of social media. And we never stop hungering for Turkish delight–sized bites of digital scandal.

"Mobile is a great market. It is the greatest market the tech industry, or any industry for that matter, has ever seen," said technology analyst Ben Thompson. Why? "It is only when we're doing something specific that we aren't using our phones, and the empty spaces of our lives are far greater than anyone imagined. Into this void—this massive market, both in terms of numbers and available time—came the perfect product."[2]

Smartphones make it possible for the attention economy to target our little attention gaps as we transition between tasks and duties. Our attention may be slightly elastic enough to fill up every empty gap of silence in our days, but in the end it's still a zero-sum game. We have limited amounts of time to focus in a given day, and now every second of our attention can be targeted and commoditized.

The rarity of gold and silver once gave substance to the worth of cash. Today, the scarcity of human attention

1. Craig Mod, Longform Podcast, "289: Craig Mod," longform.org, April 11, 2018.
2. Ben Thompson, "The Facebook Epoch," stratechery.com, September 30, 2015.

brings value to accrued likes and plays and shares. The ticks of human attention are the new social currency that determine the value of our media.[3] And that's because eventually we all run out of precious time. In the words of Satya Nadella, the CEO of Microsoft: "We are moving from a world where computing power was scarce to a place where it now is almost limitless, and where the true scarce commodity is increasingly human attention."[4]

Again, human attention is a zero-sum game. At some point we must close all our screens and fall asleep—which makes *sleep* the enemy of digital spectacle makers (and sleep was named chief competitor by the CEO of the video-streaming giant Netflix[5]). Entertainment giants win when they can keep us bingeing shows late into the night, which is why digital video giant Hulu teamed up with eye-drop maker Visine to create an ad about how the two work together to help us cram more video into our already eye-abusing addiction to screens all morning, day, and night.[6]

Our conscious attention is now the scarce and precious commodity for the engineers of digital eye candy. And what seizes the most eyes is not just the livestream of a police chase but the "snap ending" of the police chase, the abrupt conclusion—the crash, the blown tires, the blockade,

3. Martin Burckhardt and Dirk Höfer, *All and Nothing: A Digital Apocalypse* (Cambridge, MA: MIT Press, 2017), 38.

4. Polly Mosendz, "Microsoft's CEO Sent a 3,187-Word Memo and We Read [I]t So You Don't Have To," theatlantic.com, July 10, 2014.

5. Peter Kafka, "Amazon? HBO? Netflix Thinks Its Real Competitor Is . . . Sleep," recode.net, April 17, 2017.

6. Video, "Hulu + Visine View Better," youtube.com, January 30, 2017.

the shoot-out. This rush to the point was foreseen in Ray Bradbury's novel *Fahrenheit 451*—the temperature at which books burn. A generation raised on cable and remote control has given way to a digital generation conditioned to scan videos, scrub ahead, and jump ten seconds forward in search of the "snap ending." The onrush of tiny spectacles means that we must speed up how we process them. Get to the point fast, as Bradbury's character explains: "Speed up the film, Montag, quick. *Click, Pic, Look, Eye, Now, Flick, Here, There, Swift, Pace, Up, Down, In, Out, Why, How, Who, What, Where, Eh? Uh! Bang! Smack! Wallop, Bing, Bong, Boom!* . . . Politics? One column, two sentences, a headline! Then, in mid-air, all vanishes! Whirl man's mind around about so fast under the pumping hands of publishers, exploiters, broadcasters, that the centrifuge flings off all unnecessary, time-wasting thought!"[7]

Bradbury saw it all along. Behind the production pumps of the spectacle makers, and behind the curtain of social media, everything is made and watched for one thing—the snap ending. Sports become four-second clips. Movies become five-second GIFs. Politics become six-second tweets. The tornado chaser's footage becomes a dramatic twenty-second video.

Most cunning of all, the stream of endlessly flickering images delivered to our eyes is not random but driven by new suggestions custom-fitted to the fingerprint of what

7. Ray Bradbury, *Fahrenheit 451*, 50th anniversary ed. (New York: Simon & Schuster, 2012), 52.

most interested us in the past. All our preceding videos watched, shoes bought, clips liked, terms searched, shows binged, movies rented—every past digital decision, even regrettable ones—inform a digital algorithm that targets us with a narrowed offering of what will capture our eyes next. Our attention is willingly shattered into a million pieces, guided by our impulsive urges, captured into our digital profiles, and exploited by the spectacle merchants.

§13: THE SPECTACLE OF THE BODY

The August 6, 1984, cover of *Newsweek* announced "The Video Revolution." The moment marked a titanic change in the distribution of video, all made possible by the video-cassette recorder. For the first time, the VCR brought blockbuster motion pictures affordably into the personal theater of the family room. VCRs made it possible to record and rewind and replay live television on blank cassettes. Shoulder video cameras allowed families to easily capture memories in living color. And, of course, the VCR player "liberated" the porn video industry from seedy red-light district cinemas, expanding its reach into the privacy (and anonymity) of the home.

Whenever video technology advances, the pornographer's profits spike. The porn industry is the most lucrative video industry because it captures what's most captivating to the mass human gaze—a primordial urge, a desire not merely for nudity, but for bodies, objects, spectacles of lust. Pornography is as much a lust play as it is a power play, and no spectacle is more culturally potent.

The story of David and Bathsheba remains one of the most legendary stories of male power and unchecked lust pilfering the spectacle of a woman's nude body.[1] Standing on his rooftop, overlooking the city under his control, David beheld a bathing woman. Bathsheba was not relaxing in a bubble bath as part of a daily convenience or soothing

1. 2 Sam. 11:1–12:23.

comfort. Like any devoted Jewish woman, she bathed once a month, a ceremonial necessity fitted to her biological cycle, meaning she was set in the compromised position of self-touch necessitated by ritual purity. Her bathing was a signal of renewed sexual availability to her husband (now off fighting the king's war). Unknown to her, David turned her private moment of obedience to God into a spectacle of his voyeuristic lust. It makes us uncomfortable, and that's the point of the story—to stigmatize the king's adulterous gaze for the body of another.

This invasive spectacle is a prototype for all digital pornography: a woman before the eyes of an unseen man. With an endless buffet of digital pornography for the spectacle-seeking eyes, sexual lust today becomes chains of addiction that cannot be broken, apart from resolute resistance and supernatural power. The proverbial king on his rooftop, with unchecked lure of lustful eyes, has become every man and woman with a moment of leisure and the unchecked curiosity for new pornography. The web offers ten thousand bodies, ready to digitally perform, a harem of Solomonic proportion (times ten!).

"Biologically, it appears the visual apparatus is much more connected to male sexuality," says feminist Camille Paglia.[2] The lustful eyes of a man are powerfully captured by the body of a woman. The flaunted, sexualized woman is a failsafe strategy for spectacles meant to grab a man by

---

2. American Enterprise Institute, "Christina Hoff Sommers and Camille Paglia on the 'Male Gaze,'" June 23, 2016, YouTube.com. See also Slavoj Žižek, "Sign a Contract before Sex? Political Correctness Could Destroy Passion," rt.com, December 25, 2017.

the eyeballs. But the phenomenon also works relationally. "This is what women don't understand," warns Paglia; "they think they can put on every kind of sexy costume and it's merely décor, that it does not carry its own message. They don't see things as visually as men do." In sum, she says, "there's a charge in female sexuality. Young women today want to wield the power of female sexuality without then accepting the consequences of it."[3]

Without elaborating on those consequences (a large discussion and debate that will not fit here), Paglia's main point is important. Female sexuality is an electrified spectacle, and every woman learns about this mysterious wattage she employs to control the attention of men, a power that grows if she's willing to reveal more of her unimpeded curves and expose more of her skin. Sex sells, and by offering more of her body, the sexualized woman can peddle in likes and favorites on social media. The sexualized woman can peddle anything—cold beer, bubbly sodas, male deodorant, gym memberships, new cars, television shows, action movies, video games, and vacation packages. The more visible the skin, the more irresistible the spectacle. But these spectacles of female sexuality, potent as they are, rot a society's most precious institution. The smutty pornographer, the risqué ad man, and the naive woman each wield wattage of lust-awakening power with charged fallout that none of them fully understands—grabbing eyes and attention, yes, while also hardening hearts, eroding

3. American Enterprise Institute, "Christina Hoff Sommers and Camille Paglia."

marriages, objectifying the female body, and impeding the private sanctuary of sexuality necessary for marriages in any culture to endure and thrive.

On one hand, women become objectified sex objects before male voyeurs. On the other hand, women willingly objectify themselves, flaunting sex appeal as a power play over men. Both are condemned in Scripture. The Bible simultaneously celebrates the nude nuptial gaze within the marriage covenant,[4] forbids feminine immodesty in public,[5] and forbids the lustful gazing of men at the bodies of women, nude or clothed.[6]

While David's voyeurism leaves us very uncomfortable, our spectacles make us more and more comfortable as men watching the sexualized presence of women—the male gaze of lust. It is this obscene gaze of the man that degrades the woman, separating her sexuality from her being, seeing her as an erotic actor divorced from her person, a woman objectified and dehumanized by unchecked eyes of male lust, a spectacle of flesh to be used and then discarded.[7]

But the rooftop voyeurism of David is now laughable to a generation with pixilated *tele-vision* to zoom our lustful gaze as close to our object as we wish.

———

4. Song 4:1–16.
5. 1 Tim. 2:9–10; 1 Pet. 3:3–4; Rev. 17:1–6.
6. 2 Sam. 11:2; Job 31:1; Matt. 5:28.
7. See Roger Scruton, *Sexual Desire: A Philosophical Investigation* (New York: Bloomsbury Academic, 2006).

We could survey many other ways that spectacles dominate culture, but we must move on to more important matters. For politics, power, war, sex, sports, social media, gaming, or entertainment, the best spectacles grab mass attention. Our culture is no longer banded together by shared beliefs; it's drawn together by shared spectacles. Like Halloween costumes designed to match the most popular movies, we seek our self-identity inside the cultural spectacles we share together.

Viral spectacles are the new currency in the areas of social power, political momentum, personal branding, and financial wealth. Even short video clips are powerful currency—used to initiate social sway, lobby for cultural reform, generate political momentum, or stockpile economic force in the hands of the spectacle makers. Whether for good or bad, cultural spectacle is the coinage for accumulating power. Without compelling footage or a visual icon, these mass powers are more difficult to collect. But compelling footage gathers and animates the masses.

In the midst of these power plays, this buying and selling at the tables of the spectacle makers, the church is called to be separate and stand apart from the spectacles of our age so that she can ask the critical, and even self-critical, questions.

§14: THE CHURCH IN THE ATTENTION MARKET

In the long history of attention giving and attention getting, the church once enjoyed a corner on the market. But that dominance is over, says law professor and technology expert Tim Wu in his book *The Attention Merchants: The Epic Scramble to Get Inside Our Heads*. "To be sure, it isn't as if before the twentieth century everyone was walking around thinking of God all the time," he writes.[1] "Nevertheless, the Church was the one institution whose mission depended on galvanizing attention; and through its daily and weekly offices, as well as its sometimes central role in education, that is exactly what it managed to do. At the dawn of the attention industries, then, religion was still, in a very real sense, the incumbent operation, the only large-scale human endeavor designed to capture attention and use it. But over the twentieth century, organized religion, which had weathered the doubts raised by the Enlightenment, would prove vulnerable to other claims on and uses for attention."[2]

Historically, religion was the powerhouse shaping a whole culture's collective imagination, but the spectacle makers have usurped this role today. Our media reaches out to captivate our imaginations—not with a new god but with a new shampoo. Consumer products are presented

---

1. Tim Wu, *The Attention Merchants: The Epic Scramble to Get Inside Our Heads* (New York: Knopf, 2016), 27.
2. Ibid.

in pixels before our eyes for us to try on. This new ability to monetize the human gaze ushered in the attention economy run by attention merchants.

Wu's point is important, if slightly exaggerated, for the simple reason that Jesus clearly warned his followers in the first century to guard themselves from the consuming desire for wealth. Love of money was (and remains) a corrosive idolatry, forcing human attention away from the message of the gospel.[3]

Because human attention has always been lured from the weight of eternal things and hooked by the shiny bait of expiring things, the church has never enjoyed exclusivity in the market of human attention. But Wu's observation is important to see, especially as he traces the history of attention-merchant tycoons who monetized the printing press, television, Internet, and eventually the smartphone. The rise of media saturation, targeting every moment of our lives, has ushered in a new age of competition with the gospel for the human gaze.

This culture-wide attention grab is a challenge to the church in two obvious ways. First, in our attempts to reach the lost we compete with the fragmented spectacles that drain life of its sober attention and focus. Second, we lose the ability to disconnect from culture in order to flourish in communion with God. Prayer requires our divine-centered attention. In prayer, we take a moment (or longer) to consciously pray to the Father, in the name of the Son, through

---

3. Matt. 13:22; Mark 4:19.

the Holy Spirit—not just in our morning entreaties or mealtime thanksgivings but in brief petitions sprinkling divine life in our days.

Paul calls us to the discipline of prayer. We must not only pray without ceasing; we must pray without ceasing in a spirit of undaunted alertness—that is, with full attention.[4] Perhaps the best example of what it means to live a productive, ceaselessly prayerful life comes from nineteenth-century preacher Charles Spurgeon, who told a friend: "I always feel it well just to put a few words of prayer between everything I do."[5] To pray without ceasing is not a neglect of daily duties. It is not multitasking, with our attention split between God and work. Praying without ceasing claims the momentary transitions in our day, the rare empty moments of silence, and turns our attention on God himself, moments now plundered and carried off by digital media.

Prayerlessness may be the fault of my media. It is certainly the fault of my heart. In the little cracks of time in my day, with my limited attention, I am more apt to check or feed social media than I am to pray. Because of my negligence, God grows increasingly distant from my life.

Yes, there are apps and alerts to remind us to pray. May we use them. But in the digital age, nine-second intervals of attention calculate into four hundred discrete spectacle modules per Snapchat hour, a spiritual chaos meant not

---

4. Eph. 6:18; 1 Thess. 5:17.
5. W. Y. Fullerton, *Charles Spurgeon: A Biography: The Life of C. H. Spurgeon by a Close Friend* (North Charleston, SC: CreateSpace, 2014), 135.

to serve the soul but to serve the attention merchants. Our attention is finite, but our call to persistent prayer is clear. It's time to be honest. The worst of our compulsive social media habits are filling our days and corroding our prayer lives.

So how can Christians thrive in this spectacle-saturated digital age?

PART 2

THE SPECTACLE

§15: SPECTAKILS IN TENSION

The first published mention of "spectakils" in the English language can be traced back to Christian preacher, mystic, and hermit Richard Rolle.[1] In the 1340s he published an English translation and commentary on Psalms and made an observation on Psalm 40:4, "Blessed is the man who makes the LORD his trust, who does not turn to the proud, to those who go astray after a lie!" To the text, Rolle added remarks about the Christian who is "blissful" because he trusts in Christ alone, who "hopes in him, not bodily things, not earthly," and who avoids the world's vanities. The Christian, said Rolle, turns his eyes from the mad illusions of "the vile lusts of this world, as hopping and dancing of tumblers and harlots, and other *spectakils*," that make men lose their attention for God, and give their attention to the Devil.[2]

Jesters, jugglers, and gymnasts—apparently this was the trio of popular entertainment options back in the day. From this medieval inception, the word *spectakils* brought clarity to the fundamental attention-tension in this life between the world's allurements and the Christian's devotion. Spectacles compete with God for our attention.

Again, our culture is not the first to live in an age captured by vain spectacles. Even pre-mass-media generations

---

1. According to the *Oxford English Dictionary*, 2nd ed., 20 vols. (Oxford, UK: Oxford University Press, 1989).

2. Richard Rolle of Hampole, *The Psalter or Psalms of David, and Certain Canticles* (Oxford, UK: Clarendon Press, 1884), 147. His comment is on the Latin Vulgate translation of Ps. 39:5, or what we know as Ps. 40:4. Quote slightly altered for readability.

were to some degree visual cultures, which makes the question of spectacles a perennial one that our ancestors in the faith also wrestled with, as they lived by the motto: "We walk by faith, not by sight" (2 Cor. 5:7).

Long before Rolle, the early church fathers wrestled with whether Christians should attend pagan plays or join in Rome's blood sports. Tertullian wrote an entire book to define the idol of entertainment in *De Spectaculis*, a long answer to the suggestion that a Christian can feed himself on the cultural spectacles of the age with no ill effects on his faith. Of the stage he asked: Why should it be lawful to watch an actor do what it is a sin to do? How can Christians enjoy watching sin on a stage that would be condemned in the streets? He condemned violent sports that disfigure the bodies of God's image bearers. He lamented Christians who continue "sighing for goal-posts, the stage, the dust, the arena."[3] You want a spectacle to fill your eyes? "But what a spectacle is already at hand—the return of the Lord."[4] He ended the book with a punch, contending that Christians should anticipate greater delights and greater joys than those now delivered by all the spectacles of the circus, theaters, and stadiums combined.

In his *Confessions* Augustine wrestled with the same concerns over pagan plays and Colloseum carnage. He concluded that even stage dramas are not harmless fun but ice-boxes that chill Christian hearts by conditioning viewers to

---

3. *Tertullian: Apology and De Spectaculis. Minucius Felix: Octavius.* Loeb Classical Library 250 (Cambridge, MA: Harvard University Press, 1931), 295.
4. Ibid., 297.

become passive gazers at the troubled plights and needs of the hurting on stage.

The Puritans asked similar questions and worked tirelessly for decades to close London's theaters, from 1576 until they succeeded in 1642.

Christians have not always been charitable in these debates, and often they have proved themselves unreasonable and wrong in their concerns. But what I want to show here is that today, when Christians voice concerns over cinema, television, social media, and gaming, those concerns follow a long lineage of questions asked by the church.

§16: PRYNNE'S FOOTNOTE

In each generation, Christian leaders have voiced warnings over the spectacle industry. Some of their far-off conclusions we can reject. But they also landed a few punches we can learn from. One mixed example is the Puritans' fight against stage play theaters in seventeenth-century London, theaters made famous by William Shakespeare.

The Puritans opposed the theater for several reasons. Theaters drew crowds together into one tight space, and in a plague-susceptible age they incubated a petri dish of public health concerns. The wood-framed structures could collapse with too many theatergoers or become a tinderbox for catastrophic fires. Even when theaters were epidemically, structurally, and combustibly safe, theater districts attracted prostitutes and gamblers. The theaters were public health hazards as much as moral hazards, and they were attacked by the Puritans who "closed theaters not because they did not enjoy drama but because the theaters of their day were immoral and demoralizing places" both in script and locale.[1]

Among the antagonists of London theaters in the seventeenth century rose the especially rowdy voice of William Prynne, a lawyer who employed his prosecutorial mind to compile a massive case against the London stage play industry. He wrote an encyclopedic, one thousand-page, scandalous, theater-trashing book titled *Histriomastix: The Player's Scourge, or Actor's Tragedy*, published in 1633.

---

1. J. I. Packer, *God's Plans for You* (Wheaton, IL: Crossway, 2001), 84.

It would be unfair to the Puritan preachers we know from history to lump Prynne with them. He was defiant, independent, outspoken, and driven to publish a massive compendium of all the arguments he could find against the theater. At the height of Puritan animosity against the London stage plays, his provocations became a weapon— sharpened, printed, and aimed directly at everything dangerous and degenerate about the London theaters.

Again, the Puritan preachers were not opposed to the playhouses, per se; they were opposed to the sin those theaters featured on stage and attracted off stage. From pulpits, they warned against the lures of the entertainment industry, while also holding out hope that one day edifying dramas and comedies would be written and performed.[2]

But that hope was overshadowed by Prynne's prickly book, which berated actors as "usually the very filth and offscouring, the very lewdest, basest, worst and most perniciously vicious of the sons of men."[3] In one of Prynne's many footnotes, he published an insult aimed at the London actresses who worked in the popular Blackfriars Theatre, calling them "impudent, shameful, unwomanish, graceless, whorish."[4] Typeset and printed, the book hit the market about one month before Queen Henrietta Maria

---

2. "I think it possible to devise and act a comedy or tragedy, which should be lawful, and very edifying." Richard Baxter, *The Practical Works of the Rev. Richard Baxter* (London: James Duncan, 1830), 5:483.

3. William Prynne, *Histrio-mastix: The players scourge, or, actors tragædie* (London, 1633), 133.

4. Ibid.

made a celebrity appearance on a Blackfriar stage.[5] The comment was crude, the timing was bad, and King Charles interpreted the footnote as a personal offense. Prynne was arrested, imprisoned, fined, stripped of his Oxford degree, and pilloried in stocks—where his ears were "cropped," or trimmed off at the top.[6] But this didn't stop him. While in prison, he continued writing and publishing bitter pamphlets. Upon a second indictment a few years later, and before a huge throng of spectators, an executioner branded Prynne's face with the initials "SL" for "Seditious Libeler," and then fully severed off what was left of his ears with a hot knife. As a finale, the executioner exceeded his official orders, slicing down through Prynne's ears and then into his cheeks and neck, narrowly missing his jugular vein.[7] Blood-soaked, burned, and branded, Prynne was dragged from the watching crowd with one ear gone and the other dangling by a thread of flesh (later removed by a surgeon). The image of his branded and bloodied head made Prynne into a spectacle himself, an icon of ostracism so potent that Nathaniel Hawthorne would later name his famous adulteress Hester *Prynne*.

But it would be wrong to simply close the history books and ignore William Prynne for his spiked and scandalous approach, because his attack on the theater landed a few

---

5. Elbert N. S. Thompson, *The Controversy between the Puritans and the Stage* (New York: Henry Holt, 1903), 176.

6. Sidney Lee, ed., *Dictionary of National Biography* (London: Oxford University Press, 1896), 46:432.

7. William Lamont, "Prynne, William (1600–1669), Pamphleteer and Lawyer," oxforddnb.com.

good and fair punches. Perhaps the hardest punch landed in the opening pages of his introduction where he wrote this sentence:

> Let other men therefore who love their stage-plays better than their God, and their souls, resort to theaters while they please; but let Christ Jesus be your all in all, your only solace, your only *Spectacle*, and joy on earth, whose soul-ravishing heart-filling presence, shall be your eternal solace, your everlasting visible all-glorious most triumphant *Spectacle* in the highest heavens, whither God brings us all at length of this his Son and mercies sake.[8]

Notice his play on the word *spectacles*. Prynne put his finger on something worth rethinking in the digital age, and he imbibed it from earlier generations of Christian thinkers like Augustine. While researching this book, as I sat in a room full of old, moldy, and decaying books and came across this line, this sentence put words to tensions I have felt for years in our age of spectacles. What if, for Christians—especially in the digital age—we no longer live in a theater of *mutually exclusive spectacles*, as Prynne here suggests. What if we live in an age of *competing spectacles*?

---

8. Prynne, *Histriomastix*.

§17: THE WORLD'S GREATEST SPECTACLE

Into the spectacle-loving world, with all of its spectacle makers and spectacle-making industries, came the grandest Spectacle ever devised in the mind of God and brought about in world history—the cross of Christ. It is the hinge of history, the point of contact between BC and AD, where all time collides, where all human spectacles meet one unsurpassed, cosmic, divine spectacle.

The act of crucifixion, repeated thousands of times in the Roman Empire, was a spectacle guaranteed to attract attention. The nailing of living bodies onto trees along public roads was a Roman bloodsport for the masses—public and visible, not confined to the arena. Symbolically, crucifixion was the flexing arm of Rome's ruling power before gawking spectators in public. So vile was the punishment that, by law, Roman citizens could not be crucified. The cross was reserved for the public dehumanization of rebel slaves, a form of intimidation to keep Rome's large servile class suppressed, intimidated, and ordered.[1]

The goal of crucifixion was nothing short of the "elimination of victims from consideration as members of the human race," a "ritualized extermination" of offenders unfit to live.[2] It was role play, says one theologian—"the mocking and jeering that accompanied crucifixion were not only allowed, they were part of the spectacle and were programmed into it."[3]

---

1. Martin Hengel, *Crucifixion* (Minneapolis: Fortress Press, 1977), 51–63.
2. Fleming Rutledge, *The Crucifixion: Understanding the Death of Jesus Christ* (Grand Rapids, MI: Eerdmans, 2015), 91–92.
3. Ibid.

Crucifixion was masochistic participation. "Everyone understood that the specific role of the passersby was to exacerbate the dehumanization and degradation of the person who had been thus designated to be a spectacle. Crucifixion was cleverly designed—we might say diabolically designed—to be an almost theatrical enactment of the sadistic and inhumane impulses that lie within human beings."[4]

As the Gospel of Luke tells us: "the crowds . . . had assembled for this spectacle" (23:48). Scripture foreshadowed that Christ would see the masses "stare and gloat over me" (Ps. 22:17). This theatrical enactment of sadism inside the human heart drew a large crowd. And they saw a show! A man mocked, scorned, beaten, bloodied, and raised up on a tree. But they also saw creation shudder. The earth winced. The temple curtain split top to bottom. The noonday sun was eclipsed for three hours. Tombs broke open. The dead bodies of many Christians were raised to life.

The death of Jesus Christ was not just another crucifixion spectacle; it was the pinnacle of all crucifixion spectacles. For the Romans, "every cross was a mocking throne for rebels," but according to Scripture, the cross of Christ "was a parodic coronation and enthronement."[5] The cross of Christ was the greatest spectacle in cosmic history for what it ironically subverted. There on the hill of Calvary, Christ "disarmed the powers and authorities," and in his

---

4. Ibid.
5. Peter J. Leithart, *Defending Constantine: The Twilight of an Empire and the Dawn of Christendom* (Downers Grove, IL: IVP Academic, 2010), 24.

victory, "he made a public spectacle of them, triumphing over them by the cross" (Col. 2:15 NIV). To die on a tree was to die under the curse of God. But by hanging on a tree, Christ became a curse for us.[6]

In one large field, we could recrucify every one of the tens of thousands of prisoners and slaves and vanquished enemies in Roman history, or at least recreate the scene with CGI technology, but this crucified King remains in himself the grandest Spectacle.

From this moment on, God intended all human gaze to center on this climactic moment. It is as if God says to us: "This is my beloved Son, crucified for you, a Spectacle to capture your heart forever!" Or, as Augustine said in the age of Roman spectacles, "Do not think, brethren, that our Lord God has dismissed us without spectacles." No, for there is nothing greater in the world to see than this: "the lion vanquished by the blood of the Lamb."[7] By divine design, Christians are pro-spectacle, and we give our entire lives to this great Spectacle, now historically past and presently invisible.

By faith, this ultimate Spectacle is now the life I live. The supreme spectacle of the cross brings a cosmic collision with the spectacles of this world. And we're in the middle. I have now been crucified to the world, and the world has

---

6. Deut. 21:22–23; Gal. 3:13–14.

7. Augustine of Hippo, "Lectures or Tractates on the Gospel according to St. John," in *St. Augustin: Homilies on the Gospel of John, Homilies on the First Epistle of John, Soliloquies*, ed. Philip Schaff, trans. John Gibb and James Innes, vol. 7, A Select Library of the Nicene and Post-Nicene Fathers of the Christian Church, First Series (New York: Christian Literature Co., 1888), 50.

been crucified to me.[8] Our response to the ultimate spectacle of the cross of Christ defines us.

Depending on how you see it, the cross is one of two spectacles—the mocking of a faux king, or the coronation of the true King of the universe. The cross was either a tragic misunderstanding and a ruthless murder of an innocent man, or it was a preplanned spectacle orchestrated by God to display to the world a beauty unsurpassed.

The spectacle of Christ is driven home in conversion when I look back on my life and see that my sins stabbed holes in the bloodied body of Christ. He who loves me, I have pierced.[9] To unfallen eyes—and to redeemed eyes— the cross was a spectacle that this world has never, and will never, rival in weight or significance or glory.

So it is wholly appropriate for theologian John Murray to brand the cross of Jesus Christ as "the most solemn spectacle in all history, a spectacle unparalleled, unique, unrepeated, and unrepeatable."[10] Like the venomous snake cast in bronze and raised up as a healing spectacle to cure thousands of poisoned bodies, Christ's broken body was raised up on a Roman cross as a healing spectacle to revive millions of sinful souls.[11] Christ risen up at Calvary marked the pinnacle spectacle for which all other spectacles in world history will never reach, the preeminent spectacle

---

8. Gal. 2:20; 6:14.

9. See David Clarkson, *The Works of David Clarkson* (Edinburgh: James Nichol, 1864), 1:108.

10. John Murray, *Redemption Accomplished and Applied* (Grand Rapids, MI: Eerdmans, 2015), 76.

11. Num. 21:4–9; John 3:14–15.

of divine life and divine love, freely offered to the gawking world.

The axis of the cross marks the turning point for God's plan for this universe.[12] The cross points in four directions as the spectacle that brings together heaven, earth, all nations to his left, and every nation to his right. Rejected by earth, forsaken by heaven, this cross-beam held the Savior's arms open wide. Here divine wrath and divine mercy collided. Even more expressive than the global flood, the cross of Christ was a public display of God's righteous anger toward billions of sins, once passed over, and now judged in the full manifestation of his wrath in visible human history.[13]

In light of this supreme spectacle, Charles Spurgeon rhetorically asked: "Was there ever such a picture as that which God drew with the pencil of eternal love, dipped into the color of Almighty wrath on Calvary's summit?"[14] Answer: no. This wrath-bearing burden of Christ, invisible to the naked eye, is the truest Spectacle within the Spectacle, a climactic moment in triune history when the full cup of God's wrath was handed to the precious Son to drink down to the dregs.[15] He who knew no sin, became sin, became our sin, and embodied the full ungodliness of our iniquities.[16]

---

12. Eph. 1:10.

13. Rom. 3:23–26.

14. C. H. Spurgeon, *The Metropolitan Tabernacle Pulpit Sermons*, vol. 10 (London: Passmore & Alabaster, 1864), 359–60.

15. Isa. 51:17, 22; Jer. 25:15–16; Rev. 14:9–10; 16:19 in connection to Matt. 20:22–23; 26:39; Mark 10:38; 14:36; Luke 22:42; John 18:11.

16. 2 Cor. 5:21.

The spectacle of Christ's body was pinned up before the scoffing eyes of unholy men on the ground and pinned up as the propitiating, wrath-absorbing Spectacle before the forsaking eyes of a holy God.[17]

"When I survey the wondrous cross, what do I see?" asked Martyn Lloyd-Jones. "I see a spectacle that the world has never seen before, and will never see again. . . . The cross, with all its mighty paradoxes, is a spectacle that makes anything that you can think of in history, or anything that you can imagine, simply pale into insignificance."[18] And this: "We are living in an age that is very fond of spectacles, in the sense of some remarkable happenings and events, some great show. And the Christian glories in the cross as a spectacle, because the more he looks at the cross the more he sees the glory of God being revealed to him. It displays to him the glory of the triune God, God the Father, God the Son, God the Holy Spirit. He sees all that shining down upon him."[19]

---

17. P. T. Forsyth, *Positive Preaching and Modern Mind* (New York: A. C. Armstrong, 1907), 318–19.

18. D. Martyn Lloyd-Jones, *The Cross: God's Way of Salvation* (Wheaton, IL: Crossway, 1986), 60, 64.

19. Ibid., 56.

§18: IS THE CROSS A SPECTACLE?

In a book about spectacles on a screen, in an ocularcentric culture like ours, is it even appropriate to bring the unseen cross into our conversation? Can the cross be a *spectacle* for us today? None of us saw it. We now only read about it.

The issues faced by the early Galatian Christians can help us sort these issues today. The Galatian church had fallen under the spell of a false promise of redemption: Christ plus the works of the law. They were fumbling the gospel, abandoning Christ, and it was an absurd move. How could they fall for the bewitching hallucination of a false gospel, as though Christ's cross was insufficient? Especially when Paul told them, "It was before your eyes that Jesus Christ was publicly portrayed as crucified" (Gal. 3:1). Yet all the evidence suggests that the Galatians were *not* present for the crucifixion event.

So how did Paul claim that the Galatian church *saw* Christ crucified before their eyes as if it were publicly portrayed on a city billboard (προγράφω)? Perhaps he intended the symbolism of the Lord's Table, where the cross takes form in visible symbol. But I doubt this explains it. Rather, Paul's claim was that the Galatian church *saw* Christ crucified through the passionate, Christ-centered preaching of Paul. Through Paul's impassioned preaching, the cross, though far off in time and space, drew close and present. Just how visually graphic Paul got in his preaching of the details of Calvary is not clear, but we do see here that Christ's death became present to them—"so vividly and so impressively that his hearers imagined the matter to have happened right before their eyes."[1]

It's too hasty to write off these sermons as apostolic theatrics. Instead Paul's sermonic depiction of the crucifixion of Christ was a feat of rhetography (or ekphrasis), the awakening of the pictorial imagination through intense descriptive powers so that the cross of Christ captured the Galatian Christian's imagination with vivid force. Paul could only reflect on those moments by employing the optical metaphors of seeing, as though the spectacle of the cross was visually set before their eyes, even when it wasn't.

Even today, the bold and clear preaching of the cross materializes the spectacle of the cross before a congregation, for those with the faith to see it. By the Spirit we *see* the spectacle of the cross—for we *see* the cross of Christ even today through faithful sermons and books and albums when the message of the cross is attended with suitable majesty. This is Paul's intention—that we too would *see* Christ, beholding his majesty and glory.

Yet this great Spectacle remains invisible. It is a distinct mark of Christians, who do not merely look at what can be seen but who gaze into realms of unseen glory.[2] By this faith we are filled with an inexpressible joy in Christ, a joy reminiscent of the joy of the first believers who physically saw Christ on earth.[3] But for us, the cross is the pedagogy

---

1. Hans Dieter Betz, *Galatians: A Commentary to Paul's Letter to the Churches in Galatia* (Philadelphia: Fortress Press, 1979), 131.
2. 2 Cor. 4:18.
3. 1 Pet. 1:8–9.

of faith, not of sight. At Calvary, "Satan triumphed visibly, but Christ triumphed invisibly."[4] This is why Bible movies and cinematic recreations of the cross add nothing to the spectacle of the cross and too often take away from it, leaving us with graphic imagery of a man's defeat and physical torture but deflating the spectacle of its most striking glories—unable to depict for the screen Christ's divinity or his unique work as atoning priest, wrath-bearing Savior, Passover lamb, crushed servant, Serpent smasher, cosmic warrior, forerunner of the second exodus, and alpha of the new creation.

Our world says that seeing is believing, but for us to behold the deep glory of the cross, we must see as God sees rather than as man sees. We treasure what is invisible, and that is perhaps the greatest source of the spectacle tension in this age and of the Christian life. The great spectacle of Christ crucified is a spectacle for the ear, not a spectacle for the eye. For faith comes not by seeing, but by hearing.[5]

4. Thomas Manton, *The Complete Works of Thomas Manton* (London: James Nisbet, 1874), 18:213.

5. Rom. 10:14–21; Gal. 3:1–5.

§19: TWO COMPETING THEATERS

This tension between *eye spectacles* and *ear spectacles* is not particular to Augustine in the fifth century, Rolle in the fourteenth century, or Prynne in the seventeenth century. Spectacle tension has been a reality for Christians at least since Paul penned his letter to the Colossians.

The first-century believers lived in a world of wonders and feats of human innovation and entertainment, a host of cultural, visual glories that competed with eternal, invisible glories. To combat the allurements of this world, Paul preached Christ crucified—a spectacle for the soul's endless appetite. To see how he does this, the bulk of Colossians can be divided into five sections.

Section 1: Paul celebrates the central Spectacle of the universe in Colossians 1:15–2:15. No passage in the Bible soars with Christological majesty like this one, and Paul loads these few sentences with the Savior's majesty and splendor. Christ is the creator, sustainer, redeemer, and restorer of all things. In his resurrection, he becomes the firstborn citizen of the new creation. Before any spectacle existed, Christ existed. After all the spectacles of this world are gone, Christ will still reign. The glory of Christ enchants every corner of the cosmos, but the centerpiece of Paul's vision remains focused on the cross. Christ's victory is the spectacle that holds the attention of the universe.

In his prolonged death, hanging completely naked before the world,[1] Christ exposed all the powers of sin, mak-

---

1. "Victims were crucified completely naked: the cross was meant to be an instrument of shame as well as of pain. So the soldiers gamble to determine who will

ing them a public spectacle of derision. At Calvary, Christ "disarmed the rulers and authorities and put them to open shame, by triumphing over them in him" (Col. 2:15). The crucifixion may have looked like a horrific spectacle of a defrocked king, mocked as a powerless and kingdomless fraud. But the true spectacle of the cross and resurrection was a three-day conquest march of Satan and all his powers, a triumphal procession far beyond the scope of anything Rome had ever seen. The cross was not Christ's defeat but his triumph, his march of victory—like a decorated general on a two-wheeled chariot riding through the city before boisterous crowds, flaunting wagons full of foreign spoils, flying banners painted with triumphant war scenes, and parading his defeated foes in chains.[2]

In this section, we behold the invisible spectacle of Christ as divine warrior—the spectacle of power that all other military spectacles can only echo in a faint imitation. The takeaway: "Let us apply ourselves to the fruition of this magnificent spectacle, and afford it all the sense and attention that we have."[3] May this glory continually reenchant our lives.

Section 2: Paul cautions against asceticism in Colossians 2:16–23. There's a deadly humility, an overhumility, in this text. It's the idea that escaping the world and living

gain possession of Jesus' clothing (Matt. 27:35)." D. A. Carson, *Scandalous: The Cross and Resurrection of Jesus* (Wheaton, IL: Crossway, 2010), 21.

2. Richard C. Beacham, *Spectacle Entertainments of Early Imperial Rome* (New Haven, CT: Yale University Press, 1999), 19–21.

3. Jean Daillé, *An Exposition of the Epistle of Saint Paul to the Colossians*, ed. James Sherman, trans. F. S. (Philadelphia: Presbyterian Board of Publication, n.d.), 361.

outside of the presence of society and secular culture will ensure our spiritual health. But withdrawing from society is no guaranteed cure. The Christian can thrive even as she lives *inside* a secular culture with all of its allurements and spectacles. Her strength comes from where she fixes her attention.

Section 3: Paul recenters our attention in Colossians 3:1–4. Two theaters compete for our gaze: the theater of sin on earth and the theater of glory where Christ is. These divergent auditoriums represent two eschatological outlooks. In Colossians 3:2, 5 and in Philippians 3:19, Paul talks about the *earthly* "as the special theater of sin."[4] The *earthly* is the present theater that dominates the public gaze, but it represents an age that is being undone and ended. The *heavenly* is the present (and future) theater, and it represents the new creational age, which is breaking out in Christians and in the church now and will ultimately globalize when Christ returns.

Paul explains these two theaters spatially—one *above* and one *below*—but as we saw in the first section, and will see again soon, Paul's point is eschatological. Through the lens of eternity, he sees one age passing away and another age, a new creation, dawning in Christ.

To be resurrected to new life is to set our minds on heaven. Our attention continues to snap back to heaven as its default spectacle. In our worship on Sunday, our minds

---

4. Peter T. O'Brien, *Colossians, Philemon*, vol. 44, Word Biblical Commentary (Dallas: Word, 1998), 161.

should rivet to Christ. At work on Monday, our redeemed minds should return to Christ. Throughout the week— in the morning when we wake up, at mealtimes, in the evening, every day—our minds should reset to Christ. But human resolve alone cannot pull off such a task.

Section 4: Paul instructs us to kill the earthly inside of us in Colossians 3:5–11. The Christian's great problem is not Hollywood or Bollywood; it's the unchecked earthly desires that operate within our fallen selves. The earthly spectacles of lust and material greed feed the earthly desires inside us. The spectacle of the cross is an earthquake that reverberates through our lives and breaks the chains of our earthly spectacle addictions.

In Christ, we now aim to kill and root out every earthly sinful desire that remains inside our hearts. The world wants to feed those desires with its own spectacles. So I guard my attention not with asceticism but with awareness, caution, fasting, and selective withdrawal based on my own appetites and weaknesses. A sobered sense of my internal susceptibilities to sin must inform my media consumption and self-imposed limits. Until I can say, "I am weak," I will be overconfident in my spectacle intake.

In the words of John Piper, "God's primary strategy for changing us is to undeceive our desires."[5] That's what we see in Colossians—God works to undeceive our affections from the captive power of the worldly theater.

---

5. John Piper, private email, November 6, 2017, specifically alluding to Eph. 4:21–24. Shared with permission.

Section 5: Paul commands us to embrace our daily responsibilities in Colossians 3:12–4:6. Riveting our hearts to Christ does not make us careless in life. It does not call for a cognitive life that can *think only* about Christ. We must also think about spouse, kids, work, neighborhood, and church. We see this balance in the context of Colossians, even down to pleasing our boss on a daily basis because he is our earthly master (3:22). The world is a theater of appetites and desires and idols and sins, and we are walking through it like a soul walking contentedly, eyes straight ahead through the blazing images of Times Square in New York City. Our enemies are not our circumstances or our neighborhoods or our bosses. Our focus on the theater of Christ's glory complements our earthly callings; it does not distract us from them.

Christ's glory is the spectacle of all other spectacles, and its power is most clearly seen in how it equips and motivates and animates our faithful obedience in all other areas of life. It is disastrous to disconnect the glorious Christology at the beginning of Colossians from Paul's later commands for living out the Christian life at home and work. The spectacle of Christ is meant to pass through us in self-giving love to others. Every thought, affection, desire, and habit of our lives is radiated with Christlikeness as we snap back to the spectacle of Christ's glory—the central power plant of Christian sanctification.

———

In the digital age, we need this reminder from Colossians to reset our minds on Christ. This skill is anything but natural. We must first be regenerated and given new eyes to see the spectacle of Christ's unrivaled glory, where we can consciously and faithfully center our attention. The Holy Spirit redirects our gaze from the worthless things of this perishing world (the earthly theater), to our victorious Savior Jesus Christ (the heavenly theater).

Paul does not constrain our vision, he leavens it and stretches it out to the boundaries of a cosmic-sized drama. Christ was not merely made a spectacle on the cross; the cross became a shorthand reference for everything glorious about Christ—his work as creator and sustainer of all things, his incarnation, his life, his words, his obedience, his miracles, his shunning, his beatings, his crucifixion, his wrath bearing, his resurrection from the grave, his heavenly ascension, his kingly coronation, and his eternal priesthood—all of his glory is subsumed into his heavenly spectacle.

So while nothing about Christ was inherently appealing to the world,[6] everything about Christ is heart-ravishing for the Christian. His glory is the centerpiece of our daily spectacle appetites. Into every age of spectacles—from biblical Colossae, to imperial Rome, to Puritan London, to our digital world today—the recelebration and rearticulation of the glory of Christ must be set before us, over and over, and fed to our souls day

---

6. Isa. 53:1–3.

by day. Christ feeds our faith through words written and proclaimed. For the great Spectacle of heaven is now a divine spectacle for our ears, competing for our attention in a world bombarding us with earthly spectacles for the eyes.

§20: SPECTATORS OF GLORY

The worldview of Colossians refocuses our minds and imaginations, not merely to spotlight theology but to help us embrace theology for what it truly is—our window into divine glories and Christological spectacles meant to fill our imaginations and ravish our hearts. Paul has proven in Colossians that nothing in our social, domestic, church, or work lives escapes the influence of the cosmic spectacle of Christ's glory, shining like the sun with daily power to grow new fruit in the soil of our hearts.

How this works is more fully explained by Paul in 2 Corinthians 3:1–4:6, a particularly complex argument that shows how our loves and longings are radically renovated.[1] There Paul argues that the message of Christ is not merely a message written in stone or passed around on paper, which marked off the confines of old-covenant communication. In the past drama of redemptive history, God's radiant glory (mediated in the transfigured face of Moses), and God's text (the two tablets), were intentionally separated.[2] Behind a veil, Moses shared with God's people not the bright divine glory of his encounter with God but its written result, a divine text—a law, a script—etched on stone. Meanwhile, the divine glory represented in the ministry of Moses "was being brought to an end" (2 Cor. 3:7).

---

1. For the following argument, better articulated, see Richard B. Hays, *Echoes of Scripture in the Letters of Paul* (New Haven, CT: Yale University Press, 1993), 122–53; and Alastair J. Roberts, "Transfigured Hermeneutics 8—Moses's Veil," alastairadversaria.com, July 20, 2016.

2. Ex. 34:29–35.

All the dampened glory of Moses and the old covenant was exceeded by the splendor of Christ. Like the sparkling light of galactic stars made invisible when the sun rises, the glory of the old covenant paled in comparison to the radiance of the Son. And if Christ occasionally transfigured his glory before the eyes of the apostles, it was a mere foretaste of his fully manifested glory for eternal display.[3]

But Christ's transfigured glory is now felt inside every Christian heart, says Paul. In Christ, a veil is removed from our spiritual sight so that we can behold the Spectacle of Christ. He is dazzlingly transfigured before us, not in his person but *in the voice of Scripture*—divine text and divine glory now wed together by the Spirit, as God intended. We now behold glimmers of his beauty all over our Bibles, in his words, in his actions, and in all of the ways he unlocks and amplifies the old covenant. We become aware that in Christ are "hidden all the treasures of wisdom and knowledge" (Col. 2:3). No part of Scripture can be truly understood apart from the glory of Christ. He is the interpretive key to the whole.

Jesus is glorious in everything he is and says and does—but sinners are blind to it. Only in conversion, when we turn to Christ, the glory shroud is ripped off so that Christ's splendor and beauty become tangible to our hearts. Even today, veiled readers merely see an old religious book or a biography of Jesus. In Christ's teachings, miracles, and cross, the Pharisees were blind to his divine majesty. They

---

3. Matt. 17:1–13; Mark 9:2–13; Luke 9:28–36.

beheld Christ in the flesh, but they were veiled to his divine glory. They could see only in the old way of not-seeing.[4]

This new glory-beholding requires supernatural sight to the point that the Spectacle of Christ is given not to the literate, not to the educated, not to the religious, but to those with eyes of faith. The unveiled woman sees by faith, and she sees the spectacle of Christ's glory—and it delights her heart and changes her from the inside.

Blindness to the glory of Christ is the root of spiritual bondage, and our awakening to the glory of Christ is the basis of our spiritual freedom.[5] That initial conversion is like a lightning bolt of Christ's glory, opening our hearts to the Savior. Dead hearts are awakened to divine spectacles, and the glory Spectacle of Christ begins changing us from the inside. "For God, who said, 'Let light shine out of darkness,' has shone in our hearts to give the light of the knowledge of the glory of God in the face of Jesus Christ" (2 Cor. 4:6).

Christ is the creator of the first creation, and the inaugurator of the new creation. The power of Christ's radiant face unleashes the new creation inside his redeemed people. To be converted is to be taken into the new creation, which explains why the spectacle of the first moment when light blazed into the newly ordered creation works to metaphorically introduce the moment when the spectacular light of Christ is revealed to the newborn soul.

---

4. See John Piper, *A Peculiar Glory: How the Christian Scriptures Reveal Their Complete Truthfulness* (Wheaton, IL: Crossway, 2016).

5. 2 Cor. 3:16–18.

To partake of the new creation is to see Christ for the first time. And his glory changes us. "We all, with unveiled face, beholding the glory of the Lord, are being transformed into the same image from one degree of glory to another" (2 Cor. 3:18).

Practically speaking, the inauguration of the new creation in Christ splits humanity into two blocs, and these two alliances are not static but kinetic and dynamic. In the Spectacle of Christ, we are being pulled toward the heavenly theater, from one degree of glory to the next.[6] But in the spectacle of the worldly theater, sinners are unwittingly caught inside the undertow of a media riptide churning and trapping blind souls inside the expiring theater of this world.[7]

To see the spectacle of Christ requires faith. You must be given eyes to "see" glory. You cannot simply see by reading the Bible or books with the clearest possible articulations of the gospel. No, the Spirit must be working inside of you. He must give you the eyes of faith so you can "see" the grandest Spectacle in the universe, and respond by treasuring him above every other relationship in this world.[8] Faith gives sight, the power to see *as God sees*, which is to see very differently than how the world sees, which is a form of blindness.

To read the Bible behind a veil is darkness, and without glory our new life habits and resolutions cannot sanctify our deepest loves and longings. The Spectacle of Christ is our image, our icon (εἰκών), not yet for the eyes in our head but for the eyes of faith in our heart.

---

6. 2 Cor. 3:18.
7. 1 Cor. 7:31.
8. Matt. 10:37.

Paul explicitly roots all our progressive sanctification within this spectacle model. But too often we fall for life-hacks and gimmicks and forget this Spirit-centered and imagination-feeding paradigm in the holistic renewal of our loves and longings, even in the routines and habits of our lives. We humans don't merely *have habits*—we *are habits*, said Jonathan Edwards.[9] Therefore most of life is not first deliberated at the conscious level and then acted out. That's true. Rather, the only hope for the sanctification of our habits and loves is the Spirit. He must awaken his transforming power deep inside us and open our eyes to behold the splendor of Christ. So in his sermon on 2 Corinthians 3:18, Edwards can say this: "The glory of Christ is such, that it is of a transforming nature. It's of a powerful nature: it changes all that behold it into the same image; it reaches to the bottom of the heart, to the most inner soul; it is a sight that purifies and beautifies."[10] Only the grand Spectacle of Jesus Christ can reach to the bottom of our loves and longings with power to shape us into something whole and beautiful.

Second Corinthians 3:1–4:6 offers a profound vision of our sanctification by transfiguration, only possible to the unveiled, those who behold the beauty of Christ in Scripture as the great Spectacle of the universe.

---

9. "Created beings, in other words, do not have habits but are habits and laws. Edwards wrote that a soul's 'essence consists in powers and habits.'" Sang Hyun Lee's summary in Kenneth P. Minkema, Harry S. Stout, Adriaan C. Neele, eds., *The Jonathan Edwards Encyclopedia* (Grand Rapids, MI: Eerdmans, 2017), 271.

10. Jonathan Edwards, "A Sight of the Glory of Christ," in *Jonathan Edwards Sermons*, ed. Wilson H. Kimnach (New Haven, CT: Yale University, 1728), 2 Cor. 3:18.

§21: THE CHURCH AS SPECTACLE

As she follows Christ, the church is unveiled, changed, and progressively made more beautiful. And she becomes a spectacle to the world.

Christians in the earliest Roman churches were branded as scum. Society hated them for the simple reason that Christians resisted the massive industry of pagan idolatry. Idolatry was the power plant of the entire spectacle-spawning industry, spectacles that became "the very things Romans saw as essential for integration into society."[1] To resist the idols of ancient Rome was an open rebuke to the whole culture.[2]

This explains the hate projected at Christians by Nero, "the most flamboyantly theatrical of all Rome's emperors,"[3] who exploited his notorious spectacles for political capital. Christians will never forget one tyrannical example after a nine-day fire that ravaged Rome in the summer of 64. The emperor was so mentally unstable that swirling rumors in Rome suggested that Nero himself instigated the fires. To rebuff the accusation, Nero pinned the blame on Christians, made them his scapegoat, and unleashed his vengeance on them throughout the empire. His retribution was spectacular. Under Roman rule, crimes against the state were met with like punishments,

1. Donald G. Kyle, *Spectacles of Death in Ancient Rome* (Abingdon-on-Thames, UK: Routledge, 1998), 245.

2. Donald G. Kyle, *Sport and Spectacle in the Ancient World* (Hoboken, NJ: John Wiley, 2015), 332.

3. Richard C. Beacham, *Spectacle Entertainments of Early Imperial Rome* (New Haven, CT: Yale University Press, 1999), 200.

and the condemned were cast into a theatrical role before a gawking audience. For example, a fake king was given a crown of thorns and crucified naked, mocked and derided by his fake subjects.[4] In this case, Nero called for the Christian "arsonists" to be sacrificed to the gods through fire (*crematio*) and burned at a privately hosted spectacle (a *spectaculum*, as it was called), to light Nero's garden at night.[5]

Even today Christians are made a spectacle in three ways.

First, the church is a spectacle of scorn to this world. Reminiscent of Nero, John Bunyan's famous pilgrims were beaten, covered in mud, thrown into a cage in Vanity Fair, and "made the objects of any man's sport, or malice, or revenge."[6] They were made a spectacle of trash to entertain the city: rejected, mistreated, and slandered. Our otherworldly focus confuses the world. Our focus on the Spectacle of Christ rebukes the worldly. As a result, the church is "sometimes . . . publicly exposed to reproach and affliction" (Heb. 10:33). Being exposed to public ridicule of onlookers, we are "made a spectacle" by the Neros of the world. To preach Christ is to evoke spiritual and human opposition in this world, something like having the Colloseum's wild animals unleashed on you (1 Cor. 15:32). Or in the testimony of the apostle Paul:

---

4. Matt. 26:66–68; 27:26–44; Mark 15:15–32; Luke 22:63–65; 23:6–11; John 19:1–5.
5. Beacham, *Spectacle Entertainments of Early Imperial Rome*, 222–23.
6. John Bunyan, *The Works of John Bunyan* (Edinburgh: Banner of Truth, 1854), 3:128.

"For it seems to me God has made us apostles the last act in the show, like men condemned to death in the arena, a spectacle to the whole universe—to angels as well as men" (1 Cor. 4:9).[7] The apostles were like a capstone spectacle in the arena, the supreme sacrifice to satisfy the bloodlust of the world. In their weakness, pain, and suffering, they become to this world just another form of public theater" (θέατρον).

In reality, martyrs embraced their deaths with less drama. Historians believe that early Christian martyrs slaughtered before throngs in the Colloseum welcomed death to the degree that it made their killings rather boring in comparison to the deplorables who begged for mercy and were shown none, or, more spectacularly, who fought with zest and zeal to defend their lives, in vain.[8] Christian composure in the face of death meant that the martyrs publicly rejected both the role of *victor* and the role of *defeated foe*—fearless in the face of death, they stood before the mobs and subverted the whole spectacle-making industry of Rome.[9] Nevertheless, Christians were killed to satisfy bloodthirsty spectators. Historians believe that Nero had the apostle Paul beheaded in Rome during this post-fire

---

7. *Revised English Bible* (Oxford, UK: Cambridge University Press, 1996).

8. "The martyrs' compliance in their own deaths and their defiance of authority infuriated spectators. After some initial novelty value, and even with costumes and spectacular forms of death, Christians provided a rather poor show. They were not skillful performers like gladiators, so they received no hope or privileges. Their use is best explained by Roman hatred or religious anxiety, as punitive executions or propitiatory sacrifices, not by their entertainment value." Kyle, *Spectacles of Death in Ancient Rome*, 248. See also Kyle, *Sport and Spectacle in the Ancient World*, 334.

9. Peter J. Leithart, "Witness unto Death," firstthings.com, January 2013.

rage against Christianity, doubtlessly staging Paul's death as a bloody spectacle of its own.

Second, the church is a divine spectacle of God's victory over evil. Matched to the multi-million dollar CGI spectacles of Hollywood, the church's interior spectacles seem dull. But they are beautiful and profound. Each week the local church reenacts the same things—Bible preaching, the Lord's Table, water baptism—all of them faith-based, repeated, microspectacles (unlike the sight-based and un-repeated, expiring spectacles of the world). These church ordinances are weighted with cosmic influence. In Colossians and Ephesians, Paul is careful to show how the gospel-driven love and unity of local churches is a spectacle of the victory of Christ to the powers and principalities who seek to destroy God's created order. The church is the perpetual resistance movement. And from generation to generation, she displays a spectacle of God's victory to his cosmic foes, repeatedly striking those enemies with déjà vu of their defeat at the cross.

Third, the church is a divine spectacle for heaven. Paul often used the metaphor of the athlete to depict Christian diligence and gospel ministry.[10] Indeed, the church is a spiritual athletic association, competing before the audience of angels and faithful saints (Heb. 12:1–2). All those past saints, who made it through this world with their faith intact, are watching and cheering us home. In spite of the relentless bombardment of spectacles that seek to dominate

---

10. 1 Cor. 9:24–27; Col. 1:28–29.

our attention and define our identity, we gather on the Lord's Day, a diverse cast brought together by divine grace, actors of the true drama of the ages.

Despite the loud theatrical trailers of the world's spectacle-making machines, the church is the true dramaturgy of the ages. God has authored the weakness of his people on purpose, to highlight the power of his gospel. And in this weakness, the world thinks that they see something quite different from what is really being enacted. When the final curtain drops on world history, the world will have missed the whole point. The world watches the slandered church as something of a vain curiosity, but in reality the church is a spectacle of her own—a large cast collectively playing the starring role as bride in the human drama for which all of creation was made as a theater to display.

§22: THE CHURCH AS SPECTACLE MAKER?

In a world that loves visual spectacles, how many eye-grabbing spectacles should we work into our Sunday gatherings to make the church more comfortable and attractive to the world? How much lighting, how many fog machines, how much amplification, how elaborate the backdrops and stage sets and props and art and video projectors? On this question I largely agree with Mike Cosper, who said that "chasing religious spectacles only makes sense in a disenchanted world. If we've primed ourselves to live in a world where God doesn't show up, then we have to figure out how to make something happen on our own."[1] The whole spectacle industry today is driven by the God-denying assumption that he does not exist. If God does not exist, and if we are left with a God-sized hunger for wonder, then we must turn our eyes to the CGI magicians who are best positioned to feed the expanse of our spectacle appetites. Sunday morning spectacles could fall into this secular disenchantment—a lost confidence in the Spirit's activity among us.

In a culture where it feels natural to think of the church as a weekly gathering of spectators watching skilled actors and musicians and orators and video projections, John Donne's old contrast is worth heeding when he warns us not to approach weekly worship as "an entertainment, a show, a spectacle." Instead we approach

1. Mike Cosper, *Recapturing the Wonder: Transcendent Faith in a Disenchanted World* (Downers Grove, IL: InterVarsity Press, 2017), 64.

worship earnestly, with souls pre-primed and minds readied for active engagement in spirit and truth, not with the passive dreamlike escape of a theatergoer.[2] Our spectacles are intended to enchant the imagination, not entertain the eye.[3] So, again, which spectacles are permissible?

Perhaps the best approach is to simply admit that a church's use of skillful spectacle is valid only to the degree that it understands and celebrates the substance of the invisible Spectacle of Christ crucified, buried, risen, and ascended. If Christ's splendor is not at the center, then the spectacles of attraction, however intended, reduce the church down to just another sideshow for the cheap gaze of entertainment seekers.

In celebration of Christ, I think there remains a place for produced spectacles in the faith—worship concerts, March for Life, gospel-centered films and online videos, mega conferences, and the skillful preaching of our most celebrated pastors before thousands of gathered listeners.

And yet we should always be reminded that Jesus refused to be merely another spectacle maker.[4] Surrounded by skeptical miracle seekers, Jesus said, "Unless you see signs and wonders you will not believe."[5] There was intentional self-restraint by Jesus in his refusal to pacify the

---

2. John Donne, *Works of John Donne* (London: Parker, 1839), 5:275.

3. Neil Postman, *Amusing Ourselves to Death: Public Discourse in the Age of Show Business* (New York: Penguin, 2005), 121–22.

4. Matt. 12:38–40; 16:1–4; Luke 23:8–9.

5. John 4:48; 1 Cor. 1:22–25.

appetites of spectacle seekers looking for another round of free entertainment. Spectacle making is not unique, nor does it give the gospel an advantage, because, as a masterful spectacle maker himself, Satan can woo and wow the world with dazzling visual shows.[6]

---

6. Matt. 24:24; 2 Thess. 2:9; Rev. 13:14.

§23: A DAY INSIDE THE SPECTACLE

If this book sounds like ivory-tower reflections disconnected from modern life, I have failed. The weekend I began writing this book I sat in a massive stadium, thinking about the church as a spectacle on display, while attending my first summer X Games, the premiere competition for the world's best BMX bikers, skateboarders, and motocross dirt bike daredevils.[1] Hosted for the first time in my town, and in our new and shiny stadium, the event was everything it was advertised to be, a spectacle worthy of live national television.

Inside the huge stadium, the indoor football turf was removed and replaced with carefully manicured dirt ramps for ESPN's live broadcast. That transmission was fed back into the stadium on two HiDef jumbo-screens mounted on either side of the stadium—fifteen thousand square feet of illuminated LED screenspace. Everything inside was choreographed for these jumbotrons and for live TV. All the action was narrated in real time by commentators in the studio and by another set of emcees speaking to the live audience, whipping them into a frenzy for background noise as the broadcast returned from commercial break.

Of course there were giant jumps and violent crashes—men and women falling out of the sky onto dirt and concrete courses, bruising tailbones and breaking shoulders, while the audience gasped and medics sprinted with spi-

---

1. X Games Minneapolis, July 13–16, 2017.

nal boards to the competitor twisting on the ground. After the injuries, the television cameras panned back and ESPN broke to commercial until the athlete was taken away. Those injuries were not featured on television, but they riveted the silent gaze of the audience. Sights of mothers and girlfriends emerging from the ground-level crowd, running out onto the dirt to their injured loved ones, were not televised but are hard to forget.

Between injuries, memorable feats of physical skill defied speed and heights as breathtaking mid-air tricks that could only properly be enjoyed by magnifying the athletes into godlike proportion on the jumbotrons. The stunts were all branded—180s, 360s, no-foot backflips, barspins, supermen, tire grabs—all before an amped audience thirsty for another gulp of the glorious. The high BMX freestyle jumps got everyone to their feet. When the competitors finished, they immediately turned to the jumbotron screens to watch the replay, a real-time spectacle transferred into a slo-mo spectacle for the enjoyment of everyone, especially the upturned eyes of the athlete.

Occasional background biographical sketches introduced an athlete with prerecorded interviews in the competitor's own home, broadcasted to the stadium and to the competitor on the platform. Watching herself, she took her cue from the end of the video spot to step to the edge of the platform and perform once again for us all. The hype of the rising scores built from the first and second and third rounds. The final attempts inspired the bruised and tired athletes to remove all internal caution, perform their most daring stunts, and grasp for the gold—one first-place holder replaced by another, until the final competitor snatches the gold on his last run. Of all competitors, it is this last-minute champion who elicits the loudest crowd noise and triggers the stadium lights to get switched off and then on, to sparkle and flicker and return to full brightness, as the commentators yell over the roar and reach for words to elucidate the moment now already queued for the jumbotron.

Between the glory, sponsors grabbed at eyes. Commercials looped over and over on the jumbotrons during every break. Brand logos painted on every flat (or semiflat) surface. Breathable underwear from Hanes. Thrilling jobs in the Navy. Rugged vehicles from Toyota. Athletes dressed head to toe in sponsors' logos, mostly rendered down to monotone vectors only decryptable by the initiated.

Cameras roved everywhere: a spider camera in the middle of the stadium zoomed through the sky on thin wires, boom cameras swiveled on long arms, cameras mounted on helmets, each athlete with a posse outfitted with their own video equipment, official still photographers summiting dirt tracks for the best angles. The whole event was a spectacle for a hundred electric eyes, a choreographed dance of the modern spectacle industry: moments premeditated, prerecorded, scripted, unexpected, gruesome, glorious, slo-mo'd, looped, cut to a highlight reel and edited into a five-minute package and finally replayed to cap the day in a brief memorial of the spectacle dance we enjoyed together.

§24: OUR UNIQUE SPECTACLE TENSIONS

Early church father Cyprian said that the mother of all of Rome's public spectacles was pagan idolatry. Without these idols, the spectacle complex of Rome would never have captured such a central cultural priority. Ancient sports and our modern games carry similar temptations—where spectators are still drawn, "not to deeds of virtue, but to rivalry in violence and discord."[1] But our sports are less explicitly connected to false deities. Yes, our age idolizes sex, wealth, power, and sports—and these idols feed the spectacle industry. But we are not immediately faced with the question of whether it's religiously acceptable to enjoy a game between teams that represent two rival gods with a human blood sacrifice at halftime. We watch football games between teams like the Broncos and Bears and Vikings, contests of harmless icons. Our questions over spectacles are inherently different from the questions faced by Augustine, Cyprian, and Tertullian. Our questions are subtler and more individually tailored to our particular weaknesses.

I enjoyed the X Games, not because I was hardly present but because I was fully present in the moment to experience the spectacle with my son. But I was there to experience it in a way that I did not expect too much from it. Partly this is because I have no aspirations of the glory attained by these athletes, and I don't aspire to pulling off a backflip

1. Tatian, "Address of Tatian to the Greeks," in *Fathers of the Second Century: Hermas, Tatian, Athenagoras, Theophilus, and Clement of Alexandria (Entire)*, ed. Alexander Roberts, James Donaldson, and A. Cleveland Coxe, trans. J. E. Ryland, vol. 2, The Ante-Nicene Fathers (Buffalo, NY: Christian Literature Co., 1885), 75.

on a BMX bike (which would certainly end in a spectacle for others and likely be the end of my own life). I wasn't drawn to this spectacle because I can find my glory in it. I experienced it for what it was: a thrilling day of games. But I could also see through it. I walked up to the hologram of this culture's spectacle and my hand pushed through it, and behind it all, I could see a greater glory for which the glory of these athletes could only faintly echo.

Do I regret spending the day at the X Games? Not for a minute. It was an unforgettable day with my son. And as I sat in the stadium, it became very clear to me that to be human is to be wired with an intense desire to behold glory in spectacles. As Augustine saw in Psalm 77:12, our endless desires for spectacles—of art, painting, theater, athletics, hunting, and fishing—engage our interior affections and divulge the scope of our heart's huge appetite for glory. This same appetite drives the believer to see God's glory in creation.[2] Our appetite for worldly spectacles gives us a sense of the expanse inside our hearts for divine spectacles. What we do with this gaze-lust of our eyes is another thing, but to be fundamentally indifferent to all the visual glory of this world is not to be subhuman but to be unhuman.

Paul's warning to the Colossians should caution us from attempting life as digital hermits: "Do not watch!" "Do not

---

2. Augustine of Hippo, "Expositions on the Book of Psalms," in *Saint Augustin: Expositions on the Book of Psalms*, ed. Philip Schaff, trans. A. Cleveland Coxe, vol. 8, *A Select Library of the Nicene and Post-Nicene Fathers of the Christian Church*, First Series (New York: Christian Literature Company, 1888), 364. On Psalm 77:12.

stream!" "Do not surf!" Spectacles will always surround us, and many of them reflect God's common grace and his creative glory—if we watch closely enough. Athletic artistry like the X Games is not something to be dismissed quickly. "Great athletes are profundity in motion," and they "enable abstractions like *power* and *grace* and *control* to become not only incarnate but televisable."[3] We should watch with awe, but we must never watch naively. The Creator has carved out in every human soul a vast interior room for Christ's ravishing glory, and we fill this storehouse with worthless trinkets like a hoarder. Every spectacle of human glory attracts glory seekers who are God rejecters, who find in entertainment a spectacle that drives their self-crafting and their self-ambition. The world's spectacle industry is potent with allurements that can mesmerize the eyes and lead the heart toward a toxic and soul-destroying grasp for fame and wealth.

---

3. David Foster Wallace, *Consider the Lobster and Other Essays* (New York: Back Bay Books, 2007), 143.

§25: ONE RESOLVE, ONE REQUEST

So then what sports events should we attend? Which ones should we avoid? Which movies should we watch and avoid? Which television shows should we click on or off? What does binge-watching do to our souls? Which celebrities, if any, should we follow on social media? And how much time should we spend chasing viral links?

When God "put eternity into man's heart," he made the heart a capacious, hungry, and restless thing (Eccles. 3:11). Sinful longings drive the lust in all our faculties, not least in our vision—for "the eye is not satisfied with seeing" (Eccles. 1:8). Just as hell and the grave engulf and never fill up, so too, "never satisfied are the eyes of man" (Prov. 27:20). The lusting eyes of mankind feed and feed and feed and never get full. Worldly eyes rove, animated by an eternal craving, seeking some new spectacle to bring peace and rest and joy. Satisfaction never arrives, it just keeps fading away.[1] The root danger is not the sparkling world but the sin within us. Unbridled eyes roam restless over the earth, hungry for some new thrill. And until hell and the grave are swollen, man's eyes will keep looking to the world's spectacles for what they can never find. Billions of eyes will remain captive to the spectacle magicians and their latest offerings.

Complicating matters further is my own self-awareness. I know that my fallen heart remains easily captured by van-

---

1. 1 John 2:15–17.

ity. When these questions of the media age barrage me, and I am unsettled when I think of my own heart, I turn to God's Word for one resolution and one prayer.

First, the psalmist proclaims his personal resolution in Psalm 101:3: "I will not set before my eyes anything that is worthless." The term here—*worthless*—is a compound, literally: *without profit*. It is "the quality of being useless, good for nothing."[2] For the psalmist, something that is "without profit" is not simply neutral—it is evil in the sight of God. Why? We are heirs of eternal, glorious wealth, so our lust for any worthless thing is a direct offense against God. Thus, the psalmist makes the resolution, "I will not set before my eyes anything that will not profit my soul."

Second, the psalmist entreats God in Psalm 119:37: "Turn my eyes from looking at worthless things; and give me life in your ways." Again, worthless things include "anything that is unsubstantial, unreal, worthless, either materially or morally."[3] The warning here is against trusting in anything with an inherent promise that proves hollow in the end.

Worthlessness covers a huge breadth of very serious sins, starting with rebellion, idolatry, moral evil, pornography, falsehood, lies, and deception. But this category extends far more broadly. A worthless thing is something false—not

2. Francis Brown, Samuel Rolles Driver, and Charles Augustus Briggs, *Enhanced Brown-Driver-Briggs Hebrew and English Lexicon* (Oxford, UK: Clarendon Press, 1977), 116.

3. Victor P. Hamilton in R. Laird Harris, Gleason L. Archer Jr., and Bruce K. Waltke, *Theological Wordbook of the Old Testament* (Chicago: Moody Press, 1999), 908.

false as in a bold-faced lie, but inflated in what it promises to give me, something that will fail to meet the expectation it has awakened inside of me.[4] "Worthless things" fits into the Old Testament's enormous and all-inclusive vocabulary for moral evil. But do "worthless things" fit into *our* vocabulary for moral evil?

The resolve to turn away from *worthless* things is a pointed way of asking: What really brings value, meaning, and purpose to our lives? Biblical ethics is not about simply avoiding corrupting things, but learning to see and enjoy and embrace eternal things that truly bring meaning and purpose and joy into our lives. My conscience must be calibrated to Scripture so that I will firmly resolve not to set my eyes on worthless things. But I must also resolve to know that worthless things will allure me in those moments when I need God to act on my behalf.

A V-chip embedded in TVs once blacked out lewd media. Perhaps we now need a W-chip, to blank-screen worthless things. But such technology does not exist. It may never exist. We need God to turn our heads. Like a father gently holding his overstimulated son's face until he can regain his gaze, God must divert our eyes in another direction away from empty things. And we have such a Father, whom we can ask to fill our hearts with what is eternally valuable.[5] Only in the pleasures of our heavenly Father do we have hope, as his children, to turn our eyes and our hearts from

---

4. Jerry Shepherd in Willem VanGemeren, ed., *New International Dictionary of Old Testament Theology and Exegesis* (Grand Rapids, MI: Zondervan, 1997), 53.

5. Ps. 119:33–40.

worthless things, and to refocus our attention on eternal things. This is the psalmist's urgent resolve and plea: God, grab my head and turn my eyes from looking at hollow things and give me life in your ways as I behold the inestimable worth of your glory.

§26: THE SPECTATOR BEFORE HIS CARVING

The most worthless thing in Old Testament history, and thereby the most forbidden, is the idol—a carved, hand-held thing, often in the form of animals overlaid with silver or gold. Idols have carved mouths that are dumb, whittled eyes that are blind, and engraved ears that are deaf.

Idols are mute *and* idols speak lies.[1] Idols are immobile *and* idols are freighted with demonic power.[2] So how are both true? Because "its maker trusts in his own creation when he makes speechless idols!" (Hab. 2:18). So the prophets can say, "Woe to him who says to a wooden thing, Awake; to a silent stone, Arise!" (Hab. 2:19). The operative principle is not the thing itself but the creator's intent for the mute idol. Idols are dangerous when a worshiper, having lost patience in God, transfers his hope and joy into a deity represented by a handmade thing and cries to it: "Awake and arise!" In this move, human anticipation and expectation animate the dead idol into a deceptive liar. Whittled things become replacements for a seemingly far-off god the moment we implicitly expect our spectacles to arise and awaken and to grant us the joy and security only to be found in the living God of the universe. But the living God forbids his children to seek hope in dead things; he expects to be sought and pursued with all the focus and attention and affection of our hearts.[3]

---

1. 1 Cor. 12:2 with Hab. 2:18.
2. Pss. 115:4–8; 135:15–18; Isa. 46:5–7 with 1 Cor. 10:19–22 and Rev. 9:20–21.
3. Deut. 4:24, 29; Josh. 24:19, 23.

Images have always become substitutes for God, and no age makes more images than our age. We run CGI circles around the idolatry of Old Testament image makers. Even the ancient icons of the saints were less than lifelike. Our digital images are more than lifelike. "The digital medium is bringing about an *iconic reversal* that is making images seem more alive, more beautiful, and better than reality itself."[4] Our social icons are blockbuster action films, immersive VR, addictive video games, and irresistible bits on social media. Our culture fabricates a pantheon of false gods to replace the "disappearance" of God.

This spectacle tension was apparent in the Old Testament. The second commandment forbids all representative handcrafts; *then* it forbids the worship of those handcrafts (Ex. 20:4–6). This is because images, once shaped into notable form, call out for a response. Idols mediate a promise or hope or offering of joy that is God-like. Images tug at the heart by offering to complete us. Idols move the sinful human heart from craft to worship. This is how idolatry works. Idols always ask for something from us. And God is a jealous God. The security and hope and meaning and joy we look for in images can only be found in him, so God forbids the making of images because "images will inevitably take on 'a life of their own' no matter how innocent the purposes of their creators."[5] This is why forbidden image making,

---

4. Byung-Chul Han, *In the Swarm: Digital Prospects*, trans. Erik Butler (Cambridge, MA: MIT Press, 2017), 27.

5. W. J. T. Mitchell, *What Do Pictures Want? The Lives and Loves of Images* (Chicago: University of Chicago Press, 2005), 16.

like the shaping of the golden calf, feels spontaneous, almost accidental, as if the image made itself.[6]

Human spectacle making is like sorcery—an enchantment, a spell, the creation of an image that calls for a response from our inner longings. Idolatry is the original *tele-vision*, the bringing of a far-off deity close to the eyes. But God will not be brought close to his people through a golden calf. He will draw near in the Spectacle of his incarnate Son. For all the debate over how to apply the second commandment to the Christian life today (if at all), we should at least stop and ponder whether the original prohibition is not "the perfect expression of a jealous God who wants not only exclusive worship but also exclusive custody of the secret life, which means exclusive rights to the production of images."[7] Idols are forbidden because idols always demand something from us.

Jesus and the psalmist and Moses and the prophets all know the doorway into that secret life. The expanse of our soul's cavernous appetite is opened and entered by new images and spectacles that grab our hearts. The human heart bends toward what the eye sees. Today's image makers fling into the world digital spectacles of sex, wealth, power, and popularity. Those images get inside us, shape us, and form our lives in ways that compete with God's design for our focus and worship.

---

6. Ex. 32:24.
7. Mitchell, *What Do Pictures Want?*, 16–17.

§27: A MOVIE SO GOOD IT WILL RUIN YOU—WOULD YOU WATCH IT?

David Foster Wallace asks the question in his novel *Infinite Jest*—a Shakespearean title that doubles as the name of a movie within the sprawling tale.[1] Inside the story, the movie *Infinite Jest* captivates hearts and eyes in ways that no other entertainment can compete. The deadly film serves as the McGuffin for the whole novel, a plot trigger for the other subthemes.

The US government feverishly investigates the addictive movie and its effects. With his body strapped to a chair and electrodes stuck to his temple, a lab mouse of a man watches the movie, narrating to researchers with clipboards what he sees in the opening scene—"before the subject's mental and spiritual energies abruptly decline to a point where even near-lethal voltages through the electrodes couldn't divert his attention from the Entertainment." After they see the film, and then want nothing more than to watch it repeatedly, the "victims" are consigned to psychiatric wards. "The persons' lives' meanings had collapsed to such a narrow focus that no other activity or connection could hold their attention. Possessed of roughly the mental/spiritual energies of a moth."[2]

If a movie was this good—lethally entertaining—would you watch it?

---

1. David Foster Wallace, *Infinite Jest* (New York: Back Bay Books, 2006). I'm not commending this large novel to general readers. It does contain several brilliant insights into human nature, but the work is long and tedious and intricate, featuring a plot structure fabricated by a math-competent novelist and inspired by Wacław Sierpiński's gasket (a fractal triangle!), sure to frustrate many on first read.

2. Ibid., 548–49.

In a 1996 interview, Wallace called it "a kind of parodic exaggeration of people's relationship to entertainment now. But I don't think it's all that different," he said. Wallace was sounding an alarm. In the novel, US and Canadian relations are strained to the point that certain Canadian elements attempt to broadcast the movie into the US as cinematic subterfuge—an attempt to get America to "choke itself to death on candy."[3]

In the novel, Wallace managed to use one seductive film as a metaphor for America's entire entertainment industry. The US government faces the daunting challenge of warning people not to watch the film without amplifying the spectacle and exciting the masses to rush out to see the film immediately. Spoiler: it's not possible.

"I think a lot of the huggermugger in the book comes down to the fact that the government can't really do a whole lot," Wallace said. "Our decisions about how we relate to fun and entertainment and sports are very personal, so private that they're sort of between us and our hearts," he said. "In fact, there's a fair amount of high comedy at the government, going around ringing its hands trying to figure out what to do. These decisions are going to have to be made inside us as individuals about what we're going to give ourselves away to and what we aren't."[4]

3. Kunal Jasty, "A Lost 1996 Interview with David Foster Wallace," medium.com, December 21, 2014.

4. Tony Reinke, "David Foster Wallace on Entertainment Culture," tonyreinke.com, March 5, 2018.

One of the driving questions of the novel is rather blunt: Do US citizens "have the wherewithal to keep from entertaining themselves to death?" Video entertainment is going to "get better and better," he said, "and it's not clear to me that we, as a culture, are teaching ourselves or our children what we're going to say *yes* and *no* to."[5] These decisions cannot get legislated. They require personal resolve.

"I think somehow, we as a culture are afraid to teach ourselves that pleasure is dangerous," Wallace said, "and that some kinds of pleasure are better than others, and that part of being a human being means deciding how much active participation we want to have in our own lives."[6]

Wallace called himself a teleholic. He lamented the lack of self-control necessary to ingest video entertainment in small doses. He also came to believe TV was intended to be binged. So he ditched his own TV. "I don't have a TV because if I have a TV I will watch it all the time."[7] "I don't own a TV, but that is not TV's fault," he reiterated. "After an hour, I'm not even enjoying watching it because I'm feeling guilty at how non-productive I'm being. Except the feeling guilty then makes me anxious, which I want to soothe by distracting myself, so I watch TV even more. And it just gets depressing. My own relationship to TV depresses me."[8]

Some of us will have to trash our TVs, but all of us must cultivate self-awareness with our media, because Wallace

---

5. Ibid.
6. Ibid.
7. ZDFinfo, German public television station, interview with David Foster Wallace, November 2003.
8. Reinke, "David Foster Wallace on Entertainment Culture."

makes a profound (if simple) point when he says, "Most of the problems in my life have to do with my confusing what I *want* and what I *need*."[9]

I don't think that Wallace was a Christian, but he peered into profound spiritual tensions in the media age. Feeding on *sinful media* will annul your holy affections. Yes. But pampering yourself with a glut of *morally neutral media* also pillages your affectional zeal. Each of us must learn to preserve higher pleasures by revolting against lesser indulgences.[10] Our shows and movies and games lure us to give ourselves away to the screen, a video addiction Wallace called "a distorted religious impulse," a giving of the self that must be reserved for God alone, an idolatrous giving away of the soul to a media that will never love us back.[11]

Which means that the greatest problem with video gaming is not that gaming is innately evil, but that it's addictively good. Gaming taps our social competitiveness, our love of narrative, and our interest in problem solving. As gaming franchises grow, digital dreamscapes are becoming holistically immersive.

The greatest problem with TV is not that TV is innately evil, but that TV is endlessly good at giving us exactly what

9. ZDFinfo, German public television station, interview with David Foster Wallace.

10. A seemingly incongruous rivalry well captured in Neil Postman's rhetorical question: "Who is prepared to take arms against a sea of amusements?" Neil Postman, *Amusing Ourselves to Death: Public Discourse in the Age of Show Business* (New York: Penguin, 2005), 156.

11. David Lipsky and David Foster Wallace, *Although of Course You End Up Becoming Yourself: A Road Trip with David Foster Wallace* (New York: Broadway Books, 2010), 82.

we want whenever we want it. Our on-demand platforms continue to bulge with options.

We live in an age when the digital crafters of our visual culture have reached staggering heights of skill, power, and influence. They've never been better. And they're getting better. Our image makers conjure fantasies within us—not an evil thing in itself, but certainly an addictive power more appealing than ordinary life. My daily life will never compete with the tele-visual magicians of Electronic Arts, Nintendo, Hollywood, and HBO. And as our digital spectacles become more complex and textured, they make greater demands on our time and claim more of our lives.

Even when our bodies are anesthetized and we "veg out" in a dream-like coma before a screen, we are being depleted. Something is being taken from us. Wallace made a profound discovery when he suggested that our entertainment sucks away our spiritual energy. Overconsuming on amusement drains our soul's vigor. Just as my time is a zero-sum game, so is my "spiritual energy"—my affections and my bandwidth for awe.

"I think the next fifteen or twenty years are going to be a very scary and very exciting time," said Wallace, "when we have to reevaluate our relationship to fun and pleasure and entertainment, because it's going to get so good, and so high pressure, that we're going to have to forge some kind of attitude toward it that lets us live."[12]

---

12. Reinke, "David Foster Wallace on Entertainment Culture."

§28: RESISTIBLE SPECTACLES

The second commandment and the testimony of a post-modern novelist concur: the spectacles that grab our attention extract something important from us. In the extreme example, a horror film calls out from the viewer a trembling fear and a screaming thrill. Evoking fright inside the spectator is the allure of the exhibition itself. But every visual spectacle wants something from you. Take a religious example. In a Byzantine church, the visual icons implicitly call for something inside of you—your veneration, your love, even your kiss, says art historian W. J. T. Mitchell.

"Of course, this assumes pictures have a life of their own, and that's a half-life," he says. "Nobody is fooled any more than when you play with a doll, do you think it's really alive, or when you have a puppet show. But it is a kind of play that we enter into semi-consciously with images, as if they can look back at us, as if they can speak to us, and tell us what they mean or what they want."[1] Like the idol, every picture brings before us its needs, demands, and desires. "Strange as it sounds," Mitchell writes, "there is no way we can avoid asking what pictures want. This is a question we are not used to asking, and that makes us uncomfortable because it seems to be just the sort of question that an idolater would ask, one which leads the process of interpretation toward a kind of secular divination. What do the images want from us? Where are they leading

1. W. J. T. Mitchell, "W. J. T. Mitchell—A Baker-Nord Center for the Humanities Interview," youtube.com, March 23, 2008.

us? What is it they *lack*, that they are inviting us to fill in? What desire have we projected onto them, and what form do those desires take as they are projected back at us, making demands upon us, seducing us to feel and act in specific ways?"[2] Thus, every spectacle in this eye-dominant culture becomes a potential instrument or agent of domination, seduction, persuasion, and deception.

De Zengotita arrives at the same conclusion, in franker language. "Everything is firing message modules straight for your gonads, your taste buds, your vanities, your fears," he says. "But it's okay; these modules seek to penetrate, but in a passing way; it's all in fun. A second of your attention is all they ask." To live in the age of the spectacle, he says, is to live in a "psychic sauna," made just for you—aimed directly at you.[3] With so much media in our lives, we are perpetually moved by one spectacle, then another, then another. What was maybe once too shockingly immodest, or too intense for the eyes, is now made tolerable in the age of hyper-expiring spectacles. Images come and go in a sensation shower that washes over us. What's the problem, we might ask? It's all so cheap. So fleeting. Nothing shocks us. A new module of lust or gore hits and then disappears. We don't need spectacles to last beyond the shocking thrill. We don't ask them to linger. New spectacles are surely headed our way already.

---

2. W. J. T. Mitchell, *What Do Pictures Want? The Lives and Loves of Images* (Chicago: University of Chicago Press, 2005), 25.

3. Thomas de Zengotita, *Mediated: How the Media Shapes Your World and the Way You Live in It* (London: Bloomsbury, 2006), 21.

The true power of spectacles is in what *we think they offer us*. Mitchell admits, "Images are certainly not powerless, but they may be a lot weaker than we think."[4] Spectacles try to convince us that they are everything. They're not.[5] Like the ancient idols, images are active but dead, powerful but weak, meaningful but meaningless.[6] Mitchell's point is that the power of the image to make demands on us originates in the attention that we devote to it.

This makes the most unavoidable spectacles of our age the viral ones—not because those spectacles are inherently powerful, but because in attracting so much human attention they accumulate an influence over us all. Attention is the new commodity of power; the viral spectacle is the product. Which means that when we ignore a spectacle, we unplug its power. Digital spectacles share this trait with ancient handheld figurines of wood and silver. In themselves, they are powerless objects, void of meaning—until their worshipers invest them with redemptive hope, at which point they animate into idols with demonic potency behind them and divine condemnation against them.

---

4. Mitchell, *What Do Pictures Want?*, 33.
5. Ibid., 2.
6. Ibid., 10.

§29: SUMMATIONS AND APPLICATIONS

I would never trade my life for any other life in any previous era of world history. I'm in awe of this life in the technological age of cinematic glories, slo-mo athletic feats, and social media connection. And yet I know that I must live from eternal realities that call forth healthy resistance to whatever age God has placed me. This tension brings me to application. How do I thrive in Christ while I live in this age of competing spectacles? Ten thoughts.

1. Christians must call out worthless things for what they are. Spectacles often appeal to our fleshly lusts for worthless things. In any given culture, the spectacle tension Augustine saw in his day was a pull between "spectacles of the truth" and "spectacles of the flesh."[1] Our minds will be filled with one of the two. We should boldly stand up and expose spectacles of politics, warfare, entertainment, and social media when we sense that they are lies, propaganda, or flesh driven. In the age of the spectacle, few people can see through the mirage of the spectacle industry to call out worthless things. Christians can speak (and must speak) prophetically to demask spectacles as the powerless things they really are. We are called to pull back the curtain and reveal the demonic forces that stand behind the nefarious spectacles that dominate our age—especially in spectacles of lust. We must be

---

1. Augustine of Hippo, "Sermons on Selected Lessons of the New Testament," in *Saint Augustine: Sermon on the Mount, Harmony of the Gospels, Homilies on the Gospels*, ed. Philip Schaff, trans. R. G. MacMullen, vol. 6, A Select Library of the Nicene and Post-Nicene Fathers of the Christian Church, First Series (New York: Christian Literature Co., 1888), 245.

willing to consider that one explicit sex scene can wreck an entire movie, and one explicit episode can wreck an entire television series. Christians are too familiar with the feeling that our culture's greatest spectacle makers perpetually let us down. This tension is unresolvable, and we must never forget the Spectacle that guides us: Christ hung on a cross, held in the air by nails, rejected and scorned by mankind to break our addiction to every worthless thing.

2. *We must reclaim the category of eye sins.* "If your eye causes you to sin . . ." is one of the boldest phrases from the mouth of Jesus, appearing three times in the gospels.[2] Our eyes not only lead us into sinful behaviors, but also to take in sinful images. We may think of our eyes as neutral or innocent receptors, but they are not. Eyes have inherent appetites and desires. Sinful eyes rove unchecked, looking for sin. We would do well to reclaim the phrase "the lust of the eyes" (1 John 2:16 NIV) because even redeemed eyes are lustful, insatiable, never satisfied, even susceptible to spectacles of wealth, sex, power, and violence.[3] Instead, our eyes must serve as guardians of the heart. When they fail, they leave the heart exposed and unguarded. As one Puritan said, there are no means to guard the heart if we leave our eyes unguarded.[4]

3. *We must resist the manipulation of worthless spectacles.* The Puritans did not set out to destroy the entertainment

---

2. Matt. 5:29; 18:9; Mark 9:47.
3. Eccles. 1:8; 4:8; Prov. 27:20; Isa. 33:15; 2 Pet. 2:14.
4. Thomas Manton, *The Complete Works of Thomas Manton* (London: James Nisbet, 1872), 6:390.

industry. The core issue, as the Puritans knew, was not a matter of public policy, but a matter of personal appetites and desires. The Puritans were alive and awake to beauty, and they were aware of the sin inside us that is drawn to lurid appetites and to vain idleness that wastes our lives.

The soul's capacity is adaptable, and it forms itself to the object of its joy. A "steady diet of triviality shrinks the soul," says theologian John Piper. "You get used to it. It starts to seem normal. Silly becomes funny. And funny becomes pleasing. And pleasing becomes soul-satisfaction. And in the end the soul that is made for God has shrunk to fit snugly around triteness."[5] Long mesmerized by the trite, glittering spectacles of this world, our hearts cannot grow in their delight of Christ. But as we feed on Christ, his glory satisfies our hearts as it enlarges our desires for more of him. Yet we live with the tension in this world between what most captures our eyes and what most feeds our souls.

Historically, violence and eroticism are two spectacles loaded with the most potent force to shape the heart. When Jesus warns us against lustful gaze, he makes a bold statement. For many years, people have attempted to link a diet of fictional violence and on-screen sex to a rise in real acts of violence and expressions of lust. But the truth is that violent video games have not caused a rise in teen violence, and digital porn has not translated into a spike

---

5. John Piper, *Pierced by the Word: 31 Meditations for Your Soul* (Sisters, OR: Multnomah, 2003), 77.

in teen sexual activity. The more direct connection is the heart's appetite for fictional violence and sex. The problem is not that spectacles lead to sinful activity; the problem is the eye sin itself. Hidden lusts are temporarily fed by the spectacles of fictional violence and on-screen sex.

Even if a scene is fictional or even wrapped into a morality tale, where the sin is not commended but shown as destructive, those sights still have power over our hearts. As Cyprian would say of the theater: "Crimes never die out by the lapse of ages; wickedness is never abolished by process of time; impiety is never buried in oblivion," because the theater brings back all the notorious evil of history as spectacles reincarnated for the enjoyment of the eye.[6] So what becomes of our lives when the most spectacular sins of history cannot die but get endlessly re-projected to our eyes by media's latest form and packaging?

Scripture says it point-blank: the eyes that will behold the beauty of God are eyes that have been shut "from looking on evil" (Isa. 33:15–17). The spectacle of God's beauty is for the woman who refuses to feed her sensory curiosities with gratuitous gore, even perhaps in entirely fictional media. The spectacle of God's beauty is reserved for the man who refuses to feed himself endlessly on spectacular media reports that stoke personal anxiety and push God away and make him feel more distant and irrelevant to our

---

6. Cyprian of Carthage, "The Epistles of Cyprian," in *Fathers of the Third Century: Hippolytus, Cyprian, Novatian, Appendix*, ed. Alexander Roberts, James Donaldson, and A. Cleveland Coxe, trans. Robert Ernest Wallis, vol. 5, The Ante-Nicene Fathers (Buffalo, NY: Christian Literature Co., 1886), 277.

lives. In a news age when "blatant shock is the only sure-fire strategy for gaining viewers," cable news feeds our collective panic, and outrage becomes good business for the newsmakers who can "keep our collective cortisol levels [our stress hormones] high enough to maintain a constant fight-or-flight urgency."[7] Christians must guard against these spectacle tactics that manipulate our senses.

4. We must live from personal resolve. I don't anticipate that Christians in my culture will soon lead a mass revolt against corrosive entertainment, gratuitous violence, lustful ads, or on-screen nudity. My hopes for this book are inescapably tied to history.

I shake my head as I read Augustine's vain entreaties to his Christian student, Alypius, to warn him of the seductive power of ancient bloodsports. I shake my head when I read about celebrity preacher John Chrysostom, who decried the cultural lust for entertainment and particularly warned people from giving their lives to the theater and chariot races, and then, as soon as church concluded, "many of his hearers would run from his sermons to the circus to witness those exciting spectacles with the same eagerness as [non-Christians]."[8] I read about Cyprian rebuking everyone who paid to witness the gladiators, so

7. Douglas Rushkoff, *Present Shock: When Everything Happens Now* (Falmouth, ME: Current, 2014), 48–49.

8. Philip Schaff, "Prolegomena: The Life and Work of St. John Chrysostom," in *Saint Chrysostom: On the Priesthood, Ascetic Treatises, Select Homilies and Letters, Homilies on the Statues*, ed. Philip Schaff, vol. 9, A Select Library of the Nicene and Post-Nicene Fathers of the Christian Church, First Series (New York: Christian Literature Co., 1889), 11.

that "blood may gladden the lust of cruel eyes."[9] And then I shake my head when I read one historian of Rome's spectacles, who said that "Christian polemicists, notwithstanding their passion and eloquence, had little negative effect on gladiator games. The average Christian took very little (or no) notice of the critics of the games."[10] Even the persuasive powers of Augustine proved powerless to stand in the way of professing Christians allured to the bloodlust of the gladiator age. Apart from a fresh outpouring of the Holy Spirit, what hope do we have to raise a mass Christian resistance to the sex, lust, and nudity taking hold of the spectacles of the digital age? We can live from personal resolve, as we pray to the Spirit for a larger movement of the church.

5. *We must take up a martyr mind-set.* Not a "woe is me" defeatism, but a separation from this world. Chanon Ross calls us to embrace the identity of "living martyrs"—to be in the world but not of it, "dead to the world" and all its glittering spectacles and alive in Christ (Col. 2:20). To be a living martyr is to consciously refuse to live within the dominant industries of spectacles and consumerism, to strategically withdraw from the spectacle-centered and consumption-oriented world as a witness to the worth of Christ, to embrace temperance, and to recommit to the priority of community.[11]

---

9. Cyprian of Carthage, "The Epistles of Cyprian," 277.

10. Roger Dunkle, *Gladiators: Violence and Spectacle in Ancient Rome* (Abingdon-on-Thames, UK: Routledge, 2008), 201–6.

11. Chanon Ross, *Gifts Glittering and Poisoned: Spectacle, Empire, and Metaphysics* (Eugene, OR: Cascade, 2014), 109.

In this place of competing spectacles, we find a spiritual war. Satan blinds hearts by filling eyes with worthless things. His veil over human hearts today is a veil of pixels, and the chains of his spiritual bondage are tethered to the world's theater. But in a culture where relevance is measured by timely spectacle consumption, the spectacle of Christ's death has severed forever our bondage to the world's spectacle industry, this premier bondage of Satan.

As in ancient Rome, our spectacle makers find direction in the popular appetites of the masses. As David Foster Wallace pointed out, "What TV is extremely good at—and realize that this is *all it does*—is discerning what large numbers of people think they want, and supplying it."[12] The same marketing principle applies to our most potent spectacles. In a world where sex, wealth, power, and beauty are the dominant idols, these idols will flood our dominant media. The spectacle's goal is to make spectators and to keep them spectating. It's all cyclical. Video that sells is video that best mirrors what the most human eyes want. Ratings systems are set in place for adults to nurture their juiciest fantasies on screen while attempting to protect their children's eyes from those same lewd desires. But this feedback loop also means that TV is a HiDef exposé of the culture's collective appetite. TV is *imago populi*—all of a society's trendy appetites incarnated into visible form and broadcasted.[13] Today,

12. Stephen J. Burn, ed., *Conversations with David Foster Wallace* (Jackson, MS: University Press of Mississippi, 2012), 23.

13. David Foster Wallace, *A Supposedly Fun Thing I'll Never Do Again* (New York: Back Bay Books, 1998), 68.

like never before, the crowd determines *who, what, when, where,* and *why* of what appears on our screens. Crowd appetite determines our entertainment offerings.

Social media may appear to empower individual voices, but it's really the crowd's mass attention or indifference that determines which voices are seen or heard or ignored. The age of spectacles is the age of the crowd. The crowd gets what the crowd wants. If the crowd wants Barabbas, the crowd gets Barabbas. Christians can learn from Jesus's mistrust of the crowds.[14] And Christians can resist the popular spectacle trends.

The media prohibition of a previous generation—"Thou shalt not watch!"—has given way to a new law of the media land: "Thou shalt not stop watching!" The admonition to evade what corrupts us has given way to the longing to endlessly consume whatever entertains us. Limitless media production has now matched the culture's unquenchable media appetite. We are now more media obese than we are physically obese. And we are not happier. We are lonelier. We are more depressed.

Emptiness unalleviated, tele-visual values will continue to rule our culture.[15] Video entertainment is the people's opiate and escape from reality. Faced with the world's endless buffet of digital spectacles, Christians will choose to seasonally step away, to power down the screens around

---

14. John 2:23–25; 6:15; 18:38–40.
15. David Foster Wallace: "I think it would be safe to say that television—or tele-visual values—rule the culture." Terry Gross, "David Foster Wallace: The 'Fresh Air' Interview," npr.org, March 5, 1997.

them, for a day or a week or a couple of weeks. We will choose to fast from the spectacle industry, to digitally detox as a way to remind ourselves that we live in this age of spectacles as foreigners.

6. *We must not attempt to relieve every spectacle tension too quickly.* The antinomian who watches whatever he wants in the name of Christian freedom is just as naive as the legalist who celebrates his rejection of all television and movies and screen time as evidence of his Christian holiness. The spectacles of the world and the Spectacle of Christ are not friends. Sometimes they are set directly at odds (when it comes to showcasing and celebrating sin). At other times they live in unresolvable tension (when it comes to grabbing our time and attention). They will remain in tension until Christ returns to earth in his transfigured glory. Until then we are left inside the cultural pressures and given the Spirit and revelation to help us wisely walk forward in this age. It's remarkable how much wisdom a pre-mass-media book (Scripture) has to offer us in the age of the spectacle, if we are willing to listen and carefully apply it.

But we must learn to show charity to brothers and sisters when we disagree. There are no easy fixes or filters. The decision is not simply adopting everything rated TV-14 or PG-13 and under. Any given cultural spectacle must be weighed for its value. And whatever spectacles are true, honorable, just, pure, lovely, commendable—those are spectacles of substance to be potentially embraced.[16]

---

16. Phil. 4:8.

We must be cautious in condemning Christians for watching sports and movies and concerts and theater productions. Can we condemn a Christian brother who is eager to see the latest blockbuster CGI action movie? Can we give Christians room to enjoy social media or sporting events or the latest superhero movie and not question their love for Christ? Can we recognize that others may partake in the spectacles of the age without necessarily forfeiting their spiritual vitality?

On the other side, should a Christian feel out of touch when his Christian friends are laughing over the blockbuster show they binged last week? Some Christians will withdraw from many cultural spectacles. And can we blame them? Can we chide them for having an awareness of their own hearts? Or can we become Christians of maturity, who don't mock but admire those who withdraw themselves from the boldest spectacles of culture, and who postpone their senses for a future glory?

The promise is the same for us all: Blessed are the pure in heart, for giving their attention to what is holy, for their attention shall be satiated by a sight of God himself.[17] Each of us must reckon with this radical eschatological promise of Christ in our personal media diets.

At the same time, we are dealing with spectacles at amplified levels that out-saturate the temptations of the first-century world. Pagan art, spiritual architecture, cultural banquets, theater productions, Olympic games, and blood-

17. See Matt. 5:8.

sports for the masses—no matter what the first-century Roman world offered by way of eye candy, our age of screens and digital media offers to a near infinite degree. Multiple arenas in every city, live-streaming video, on-demand entertainment, and breaking media can now fill every moment of our days (and nights) unless we actively resist this competition for our gaze. No age has ever lived in the age of the spectacle like we live in the age of the spectacle. And as corporations wage war on our sleep patterns, the chief enemy of their greater profits, our zero-sum attention will continue to be targeted with even more eccentric spectacles.

7. Regularly put yourself before God's spectacle banquet. In the frenetic pulse of electric stimulation, our media overwhelms our senses, and God's wonders around us simply disappear. While Christ is the supreme Spectacle, and we find a lifetime of his glory to be discovered in Scripture, he's not the only divine spectacle. The local church is where we go to find the Lord's Table and baptism and the preaching of the Word, where those repeated spectacles call us again and again for a response of worship and repentance and joy. And we should put ourselves often before God's spectacles in creation. Creation spectacles also demand a response, for our worship and awe and gratitude to the Creator in the face of his awesome power and majesty.[18] Nature documentaries are tele-visual gifts to bring us into the habits and movements of animals, and to bring our eyes close to the astonishing places around the world we cannot

---

18. Rom. 1:18–23.

see in person. We were made to experience awe—and God's creation is eager to magnify the Creator in our eyes. But we must also escape screens and stand on the porch in a thunderstorm—watch for lightning, count the seconds between *flash* and *boom*, measure off the span by which it missed, and be amazed at the display of God's power.

8. Relationships change the spectacle conversation. Too often we abuse our spectacles in order to buffer ourselves from others. Like the Simpsons on the living room couch with eyes straight ahead, video makes it easy to overlook and even ignore the people sitting right beside us. We sedate ourselves with media to re-deaden the sting of our loneliness, even while sitting side by side with another.

Certain spectacles can also introduce a higher purpose to sporting events and theater productions and movies, opening new doors to engage a friend or spouse or child for the purpose of listening and loving and fellowship. There is a place for spectacles when you intend to use them to love another. Christians can see divine purposes beyond the spectacle. The visual spectacle is not the end, but a potential means of entering the life of another—a point of common venture, a new doorway to knowing and being known in a relationship.

We must be vigilant to discern the spectacles consumed alone in the dark, the movies watched on a single phone, and games played on a solo device. When we watch a spectacle with others, we help one another discern worthless spectacles, and we position ourselves to engage in fellowship.

9. *Discipline yourself in the supernatural act of Christ-spectating.* In his criticism of the Puritans who closed down the London theaters, G. K. Chesterton claimed that they operated from a fatal flaw. "Puritanism has not been able to sustain through three centuries that naked ecstasy of the direct contemplation of truth," he wrote; "indeed it was the whole mistake of Puritanism to imagine for a moment that it could."[19] This naked ecstasy of the direct contemplation of truth, as Chesterton put it, was not the invention of some failed Puritan ideal; it originated in Pauline imperative—a double command. If we have been raised to new life in Christ, we are commanded to "seek the things that are above, where Christ is," and then we are commanded to set our "minds on things that are above, not on things that are on earth" (Col. 3:1–2).

This direct contemplation of truth—this naked ecstasy—is a direct gaze. The mind is not merely a computer for data processing; it's the faculty for seeing. Of course Paul meant seeing in Scripture. But our gaze is direct. Our Object is real. These commands are not optional, and the Puritans never thought they were.

Those same Puritans made good use of the Latin phrase *omnis vita gustu ducitur*—every life is led along by its tastes. They knew that each creature is piloted by an inner yearning for its favorite food. Every palate is directed by an intuitive, native relish. Our natures must be completely changed

---

19. G. K. Chesterton, *Collected Plays and Chesterton on Shaw*, vol. 11, Collected Works of G. K. Chesterton (San Francisco: Ignatius Press, 1989), 381.

and renewed by grace if we are to have a taste for Christ. Only when he becomes sweet to us can we be freed from the mass appetites of the world's pleasures. The sweetness of sin must be spoiled by a new savor. The pleasure of Christ kills the old pleasures that led us, but only after we get a new, instinctive taste within us.[20]

United to the death and resurrection of Christ, Christ claims us and takes up residence at the very center of our being.[21] He changes everything. He awakens our appetite for God. And if this Christ-centered spectacle seeking seems unnatural, that's because it is supernatural in every way. "*If then you have been raised with Christ, seek the things that are above, where Christ is*" (Col. 3:1). That's a huge *if-then*. The appetite to seek after Christ in heaven is an exclusive gift from a sovereign God. Only resurrected souls will ever find their awe-appetite calibrated by the unseen Spectacle of Christ.

In this life, then, the corruption of pop entertainment is not often direct, but indirect, not merely in revealing too much, but in failing to show enough. Our movies and television dramas present a view of the world where God is inconsequential. Thus pastor David Platt's warning is necessary: "You don't become like Christ by beholding TV all week. And you don't become like Christ by beholding the Internet all week. You don't become like Christ when you fill your life with things of this world. You become like

20. Thomas Goodwin, *The Works of Thomas Goodwin* (Edinburgh: James Nichol, 1861), 3:480, 6:465–66, 10:118–19.
21. Gal. 2:20.

Christ when you behold the glory of Christ, and you expose your life, moment by moment, to his glory," all through God's revelation in Scripture.[22]

In setting our minds on the Spectacle of Christ, we are called to a personal discipline that is entirely foreign to this world, even foreign to our own natural inclinations. We learn a new divine speech—a foreign language of unseen glory—as Scripture feeds our new appetites for the Savior. Our new appetite directs us *toward* Christ. No other factor more distinguishes the Christian's appetite from the world's appetite for manufactured spectacles.

10. Speak grace to a suffering world. The spectacle of Christ's suffering gives us more than an object for the eyes of faith; it gives us relevance as we minister grace in the age of mass spectacles of suffering.

New media opens our gaze to every spectacle of tragedy and injustice across the globe—like those who suffer social injustices, who are victimized by the power players in society, or who are bullied. Grace opens our eyes to see suffering, to reach out to the oppressed and the needy, and to serve them with compassion.[23]

The spectacle of the cross unlocks new empathy from us to the latest victims in the news (both those who are seen and unseen by cameras). Christian love is never merely humanitarian sentiment; Christian love is always rooted in the cross. Even today, the church speaks empathetically, not

---

22. David Platt, "Unveiling His Glory," sermon, March 16, 2008, radical.net.
23. Matt. 25:31–46.

because she's politically "woke," or tuned in to the groaning frequency of suffering in this world, but because she regularly tastes the bitter sting and the sweet fruit of the Victim at the Lord's Table. Watching a theatrical depiction of the cross on a stage or in a film may move us powerfully in a moment, but the Lord's Table, the subtle and simple symbolism in bread and cup, calls us to engage with an imaginative power that enacts something deeper than visceral response. The Lord's Supper is a ceremony that feeds the interior affections of our hearts and the imaginative meditations of our minds, equipping us for another week of love for others and gaze-setting on Christ.[24] Christ as the center of life is the highest exhibition of the imaginative powers God has given us. And in this repeated, relived bitterness of Christ's death, his suffering is brought nearer to us, so that the church can speak a word of hope to a suffering world. Lingering long on the spectacle of the cross awakens us to injustices, gives us fresh words to speak, and renews our energy to serve.

24. Henry Scougal, *The Works of the Rev. H. Scougal* (London: Ogle, Duncan, 1822), 204.

§30: MY SUPREME CONCERN

Our calling today is not to shut down professional athletics, like the early Christians who sought to end the bloodsports of Rome. Nor is our calling to shut down Hollywood studios, like the Puritans who shut down London theaters. We are called to recognize what is worthless and develop personal disciplines to resist the impulse to fill our lives with vain spectacles.

In sum, all my concerns are dwarfed by this one: boredom with Christ. In the digital age, monotony with Christ is the chief warning signal to alert us that the spectacles of this world are suffocating our hearts from the supreme Spectacle of the universe.

As Wi-Fi capacity expands, phone screens become sharper, televisions grow larger, small theaters claim the heart of our homes (in prominence, price tag, and priority), and we begin to live inside the world of our images. And while no spectacle in this world is like *Infinite Jest* or Medusa's head—one sight and we go comatose or turn to stone—over time, spectacles taken in unwisely will make our hearts cold, sluggish, and dull to unseen eternal delights.

And if any word of this book appears to be pushing some form of media legalism, let me be clear: the Holy Spirit does not convict us of our failing and faltering in this age of intrusive media so that we will sink into a marsh of despondency or get stuck in the sludge of perpetual guilt. Yes, we've all been digitally stupid with our time and attention. But the message of the cross tells us that we are free in Christ to live for something greater! We are free to center our lives on him, to enjoy him, and to glorify him by fixing our attention on things above, where we find our superior Spectacle, our greatest treasure.

Yes, we were made for play, made to laugh, made to sport, made to enjoy one another. But our play is always healthiest when our play is parenthetical, a slice of life shared with others. In the age of the spectacle, play becomes both boundless and isolating. Everything "fun" becomes mediated amusement, eye candy pushed into our conscious realm without end. Television, sex, politics, gaming, ads, social media, sports—new spectacles endlessly erupt, spill over play's parameters, and submerge our entire conscious lives under the deluge of their totalizing aspirations. When we don't resist, when we cave to the subsidized interests of the spectacle makers, our lives become one endless carnival.[1]

Soul boredom is a great threat, and when our souls become bored, we make peace with sin. New distractions, which promise to temporarily alleviate our boredom, hover in our ethical blindspots. Media discernment forces us to directly face our soul's monotony. Calling out to our boredom, this media carnival, this surplus of digital stimuli, makes us indiscriminant with our hearts. Each of us must give ourselves away to someone or something. But in this media age, our loves and affections are frozen by the ice of

1. Umberto Eco, *Turning Back the Clock: Hot Wars and Media Populism* (Wilmington, MA: Mariner, 2008), 71–76.

vain amusements. Our hearts harden as we become nothing but consumers to be manipulated by the spectacle makers. We get trapped inside the age of spectacles, and we cannot give our lives away. Whoever would make himself a BFF of digital spectacles makes himself an enemy of God.[2]

The Christian's high calling is to guard the heart and its loves and desires.[3] The worst trade in the universe is playing in the shallow pools of the world's spectacles instead of diving deep for the treasure of eternal worth. In the face of whatever new media gets invented and popularized, and whatever questions get raised by contemporary spectacle making, in our age—and in *every age*—our lives must be anchored to Christ by this jealous urgency. "The deepest possible pleasures available to mankind are found in Christ Jesus," says pastor Matt Chandler. "We must be very serious about pursuing joy—not cheap, transient, here-for-a-moment-and-gone-the-next-moment joys—but eternal, soul-saturating, life-transforming joys."[4] As followers of Christ in the media age, as we try to discern *how much* and *how far*, we center our lives on the glory of Jesus Christ.

The Christian's battle in this media age can be won only by the expulsive power of a superior Spectacle. Christ is our safety and our guide in the age of competing spectacles, the age of social media. He is our only hope in life and death, in the age to come, and in this media age.

---

2. James 4:4.

3. Prov. 4:23.

4. Matt Chandler, "Recovering Redemption—Part 11: Persevering in the Pursuit of Joy," youtube.com, November 10, 2013.

§31: A BEAUTY THAT BEAUTIFIES

Susan Boyle was an unemployed and unremarkable forty-seven-year-old villager from Scotland who walked on a glossy stage on the TV show *Britain's Got Talent* and declared to the world that she aspired to fame as a professional vocalist. The judges scoffed in disbelief as they sat back, disinterested.

Then she performed.

Within seconds of singing the opening line to "I Dreamed a Dream," jaws dropped in the auditorium. Ten million live viewers were astonished. The video of her performance spread virally, immediately. It has since been viewed online hundreds of millions of times. "Watch the video again of Miss Boyle's performance," writes music professor and composer Michael Linton, "but this time watch the judges. There comes a time when about two-thirds through the song they are transformed. The boredom, cynicism, professionalism, even their age, all seem to be washed away. . . . Seeing the faces of [Simon] Cowell, [Amanda] Holden, and Piers [Morgan] as they listen to Miss Boyle is to see people almost beatified," he writes. "This event, the music, the words, the woman, the judges' recognition of their own shame at misjudging her (and all those other ladies in their pasts whom they similarly dismissed), sensing shame of the audience and hearing their cheers—through all of this the beauty of Boyle's singing hovers like a benediction over them. For a moment, only a moment, we glimpse them as they most fully are: generous, happy, blessed, the way God sees them. . . . And they are deeply, magnificently, beautiful."[1]

Beautiful spectacles make others beautiful, even if only for a passing moment. And this temporary benediction resembles a profound dynamic for God's children. All of the Christian life orients to a spectacle of beauty that will make us fully and completely beautiful, as God sees us and designed us to be. In Christ, we are beatified into a spectacle of permanence, a spectacle of our supreme happiness.

---

1. Michael Linton, "Beauty and Ms. Boyle," firstthings.com, April 20, 2009.

§32: THE VISIO BEATIFICA

Consolidate every display of beauty in this world into one single object and it would be the greatest spectacle on earth. And yet it would be merely a faint echo of what it means to behold the source of all beauty, the living God— the great, beautiful, eye- and soul-ravishing Spectacle of eternity.[1]

But we must wait. Right now, in the sensorium of faith, the ear is chief. Later, in the sensorium of eternity, the eye shall become chief. We live inside this tension as we hope for something greater. As Christians, we live in this present world, but we are driven by an eschatological future, the glory of a heavenly theater. In pushing away from our eyes all sinful enticements and worthless things in this world, we manifest a faith-filled longing for the day when we shall see God (*visio Dei*) and gaze on Christ with our physical eyes (*visio oculi*).[2] This vision to come—this *beatific vision*—will be the full sight of Christ in the matchless splendor of his radiance.

Christ momentarily transfigured himself before the eyes of the apostles,[3] and we are being sanctified by his transfigured glory in Scripture, but there is to come a future spectacle of manifested beauty so powerful that it will beautify us—entirely and instantly. Fully manifested before our eyes, the Lord Jesus will complete our sanctifica-

---

1. Jeremiah Burroughs, *The Saint's Happiness*, Dutch Church, Austin Friars (London, 1660), 424.
2. Matt. 5:8; 1 Cor. 13:12; 1 John 3:2.
3. Matt. 17:1–13; Mark 9:2–13; Luke 9:28–36.

tion, restore our full humanity, and purge us of everything fallen and flawed and ugly within us. This sight of Christ will fill our souls with joy, eternal happiness, and pleasures forevermore.[4]

We were made for this sight. All the vain hopes we've harbored in our consumer goods, cosmetics, diets, and the be-spectacled promises of our ad makers—all the vain hopes we've chased to mold our identity with the right features and options and choices—left us only more disenchanted in our attempt to self-craft our personal blobs. And unlike the glow of Moses's face, in this sight of the Savior's radiant appearance we shall be so thoroughly irradiated by divine glory that we will forever radiate him as his fully restored image bearers. From the first moment when we behold the permanently transfigured Christ, the great glory-Spectacle of cosmic history, we will carry within us the manifestation of Christ's beauty as our own.

In our brokenness we long for this day, to be made beautiful and whole in the indescribable presence of Christ. But again, this moment has already been unleashed inside of us, for, as Goodwin says, "faith is the introduction to the beatifical vision."[5] Or as Edwards says, the knowledge of Christ right now is "the sweetest and most happifying" thing in this life. "Other knowledge may be entertaining, but this is a light that is a spring of everlasting happiness.

---

4. Ps. 16:11.
5. Thomas Goodwin, *The Works of Thomas Goodwin* (Edinburgh: James Nichol, 1861), 21:24.

'Tis the beginning of the beatifical vision."[6] Yes, Christ's beauty has commenced before our eyes of faith, and it is making us beautiful now. To catch occasional glimpses of Christ's splendor in Scripture is to receive a beam of that beatific vision, already transforming us "from one degree of glory to another" (2 Cor. 3:18). In him we find the object of our highest love, our most secure identity, and our most anticipated Spectacle.

But this remains the age of digital images, and the spectacle industry is a gatling gun firing at us new media modules nonstop. We live inside this media age in a state of expectation as we learn to deflect those modules in anticipation of a greater Sight. This world hardly knows what it means to live in the hope of a spectacle. The world knows a ceaseless appetite to gorge on new spectacles, or a brief anticipation between the trailer and the movie, but only the Christian finds true hope in a future spectacle. For who hopes for what he sees?[7] True hope makes us patient in an ocularcentric world impatient for new sights. We don't fit in. We walk by faith and not by visual spectacles, with a hope that even now works to purify us.[8]

Step by step, we walk in faith toward Christ and toward this moment of beatific vision. The spectacle of the radiant glory of what we will become is now invisible, and we await

6. Jonathan Edwards, "One Thing Needful," in *Jonathan Edwards Sermons*, ed. Wilson H. Kimnach (New Haven, CT: Yale University, 1731), sermon on Luke 10:38–42, n.p.

7. Rom. 8:24.

8. 1 John 3:3.

the unveiling. Into the spectacle tension of this world, we live by faith, knowing that the permanently transfigured Christ, now unseen, will be revealed to our eyes, and our faith-delight in him now will give way to a ravishing sight-delight to enjoy for all of eternity.[9]

---

9. 1 Pet. 1:3–9.

§33: DIS-ILLUSIONED BUT NOT DEPRIVED

As I finished typing this book, a notification in the corner of my screen flagged my attention to an email promo from the local science museum, grandly proclaiming that its movies are now "projected on a 90-foot domed screen that wraps around and above you." That's our world, the race to enfold us in spectacles. VR has done it—wrapping our images around, behind, above, and under us. Perhaps one day an immersive world will open to us inside a VR game that will become an escape from the broken world around us. Our dystopian sci-fi novelists have already played out this possibility.[1] Our programmers may soon make it a reality—a virtual reality—a transhuman utopia where our conscious life can express itself in a customized avatar freed from race and age and gender and body type, every edge of our embodied life being overwritten by personal preference as we self-sculpt a cyber image for an entirely digital world in which we live and move and have our being.

Whatever entrancing spectacles are to come, Boorstin's warning from sixty years ago stands. We are the most

---

1. "The skyrocketing cost of oil made airlines and automobile travel too expensive for the average citizen, and the OASIS became the only getaway most people could afford. As the era of cheap, abundant energy drew to a close, poverty and unrest began to spread like a virus. Every day, more and more people had reason to seek solace inside Halliday and Morrow's virtual utopia. . . . Before long, billions of people around the world were working and playing in the OASIS every day. Some of them met, fell in love, and got married without ever setting foot on the same continent. The lines of distinction between a person's real identity and that of their avatar began to blur. It was the dawn of a new era, one where most of the human race now spent all of their free time inside a videogame." Ernest Cline, *Ready Player One: A Novel* (New York: Crown, 2011), 59–60.

illusioned people in world history. We already live inside of our illusions. Our spectacles have become a landscape around us, a concentric dome to confine our gaze in every direction. Like never before, we live inside our world of spectacles, and we sway sovereign power over the spectacles we choose to surround ourselves with. We, the spectators, have become self-governing over our ocular lives. But this worldly theater is holographic. It minimizes reality with images that attempt to constrain us to the parameters of the mass gaze, visual hopes, and collective appetites.

Our age offers limitless spectacles. But with unceasing options, the most solid eternal realities get washed away, and our lives become emptied of vision, purpose, and eternal direction. In contrast to this age stands one supreme Spectacle, Jesus Christ, the author of the universe, the core of reality, the center of our lives, and the perfecter of our human nature. Though now unseen, he calls for our deepest trust and highest affections.[2]

In Christ we reclaim our attention and push back the attention merchants. We redeem the time by reclaiming our attention.[3] We are reminded that anything done apart from faith in Christ is illusory—it has no lasting value, it is pure image, it is only ephemeral, and it will soon come to nothing.[4] So we push through the ocular realm of our age, through all the projected images, knowing that a more glorious optical reality awaits us. I have been crucified

---

2. Matt. 10:37.
3. Col. 4:5 (KJV).
4. Rom. 14:23; 2 Cor. 4:17–18.

with Christ, so I have been crucified to this earthly world of vain spectacles. And this whole expiring world of worthless spectacles has been crucified to me. When we turn our attention to Christ—our ultimate Spectacle—all the flickering pixels of our culture's worthless things and beloved idols grow strangely dim. Looking past the scintillating sights that consume this ocularcentric world, we hope for the Spectacle that we now can only see in glances and glimmers but one day will see in the splendor of his fully transfigured form, in full sight before our eyes.[5]

Like a smartphone screen made blank by the rays of direct sunshine, one day we shall see Christ's face. On that day, all the vain spectacles in this world of illusions and all the pixelated idols of our age will finally and forever dissolve away in the radiance of his splendor.

---

5. 1 Cor. 13:12.

Also Available from Tony Reinke

Do you control your phone—or does your phone control you?

Reinke identifies twelve potent ways our smartphones have changed our lives—for good and ill—and calls us to develop healthy habits for life in the digital age.

"This is a necessary book for our generation, to remind us that our phone habits will either amplify or get in the way of our most important longing of all: the soul-satisfying glory of our Savior."
JACKIE HILL PERRY, *poet; writer; hip-hop artist*

"Informed. Fair. Attentive to subtleties. Theologically insightful. This is a book very few people could have written."
JOHN PIPER, *Founder, desiringGod.org; Chancellor, Bethlehem College & Seminary*

For more information, visit **crossway.org**.